CLICK

Enjoying Friendship for New Reasons and Seasons

By Beth Jones

Harrison House

Click: Enjoying Friendship for New Reasons and Seasons
ISBN 13: 978-160683-389-6
Copyright © 2015 by Beth Jones
www.jeffandbethjones.org

Published by Harrison House Publishers
Tulsa, OK 74145
www.harrisonhouse.com

CONTENTS

CHAPTER 1
Friendship Realities

Relationships. People. Girlfriends. Remember these friendships: Lucille Ball and Ethel Mertz, Betty and Veronica, Mary Ann and Ginger, Wilma and Betty, Rachel, Monica and Phoebe, and Oprah and Gayle? How about Bible pals Ruth and Naomi and Mary and Elizabeth?

Girls and friendship are like peanut butter and jelly; they just go together! *"Make new friends but keep the old, one is silver and the other's gold."* We sang this song in Girl Scouts, but little did we know how true those words were. There's oxygen and there's friendship!

What would a café, coffee or shopping trip be like without a girlfriend? How do you survive a carpooling crisis without a friend? Who do you call when you need prayer? Who do you share your extra 10,000 words a day with? Without girlfriends, life would be so . . . so . . . so full of testosterone! We love our men, but boys are not girls. As one person said, "Girls talk, therefore we are friends."

How I Learned This Lesson

It's been said that some friendships are for a reason, a season, or a lifetime. As long as I can remember, my life has been filled with girl friendships. Here's my story. It started with my mother, who has been a friend and confidant for the largest chunk of my life. Her sense of humor, positive outlook on life and "can do" attitude made her fun to be around. I'm the oldest of four girls, so my three sisters and I have always been friends. Although we fought like sisters can in our teen years, we have always been close and kindred. In our early teens, my dad left my mother and after their divorce, our home became an estrogen-filled chick house! We learned how to talk, listen, cry, laugh, fight, forgive, steal each other's clothing—and love each other through thick and thin.

Andi and Laurie were the first "non-sister" girlfriends I remember. I was the new student at Winans Elementary, and my biggest fear as a third grader was that I wouldn't make any new friends. Andi and Laurie lived in my neighborhood and we were all in Miss Earhart's class. When they invited me to their Brownie troop, I knew I was in the group! What began in third grade continued through high school and college, and turned out to be a real divine connection, a God-knit friendship.

In junior high and high school, the gang grew. Thirteen girls plus me made up our group. We have history—Girl Scout camp, boy crushes, toilet papering neighborhoods, sleepovers, supposed séances where we tried to revive Abraham Lincoln from the dead and asked him to blow out the candle in the room, stealing cigs from our parents, getting drunk at lunch and high on the weekends, being mall rats, making fake IDs, playing sports, running student council and somehow getting good grades. We bonded. I hate to tell you, but we were the kids every Christian parent hopes their children don't hang out with! Of course, this was before I met Christ.

At the end of our senior year of high school, Andi, my friend since third grade, had a life-changing encounter with Jesus Christ as her personal Lord and Savior. It was dramatic! Our whole group thought she had flipped. Andi and I roomed together our freshman year in college and although I was the "fish" that fought all the way to the boat, it was Andi who led me to the Lord. Somewhere during the past few decades, several of us in the group have had definite, supernatural experiences with the Lord, and Jesus has taken center stage of some of our lives. Even today, although it's a bit harder with everyone's busy life, we still try to get together once a year. We rehash the old days, we notice a few more wrinkles, and we are thankful for the season of friendship we've had over the years.

Into college and young adult life, Michelle and Mary Jo were my bosom buddies and confidants. As a born-again Christian, friendships took on a whole new dimension. Jesus was the glue that held our friendship together. We shared, laughed, grew in our faith and prayed about the good, the bad and the ugly. Michelle was the first "Jonathan-David" type friend I had, so when she moved to Florida after college, the Lord brought Mary Jo into my life for another rich "Jonathan-David" friendship season.

You know how it goes. We all got married, started families, and the busy pace of life took off! Friendships went to the back burner, the letters and phone calls were more spaced out, and girl-times became a sweet memory.

My husband, Jeff, and I enjoyed our newly married life and cultivating this new world of being best friends with one another by doing everything together. We had four babies in six years and pioneered and pastored a growing church. Life was busy, busy, busy! My girl friendships were nil.

One day, thirteen years into my marriage, although I loved my husband dearly, I was longing for a friend to just go do "girl stuff" with. It was during this time that I had a major revelation—I had sown a friendship famine. What I mean is this: I had not planted any real lasting friendship seeds, I had not invested my heart in any new personal friends and the result was that I didn't have any. Yes, I had lots of acquaintances and since we were pastoring a church, there were lots of wonderful Christian girls who had become casual friends in my world, but I had not really connected with any long-term heart friends.

> **NUGGET:** In certain professions, some women find it is difficult to find the balance between professional relationships and friendships. This was true for me. I found that it was sometimes difficult to find a friend because of the various hats I wore. It could sometimes be confusing to be friends with gals in the church, since on one hand I was a pastor and spiritual leader and mentor to them, and on the other hand I was the "let your hair down" friend. Often, it's not possible to be both. Particularly if you are a pastor's wife, you know how tough this can be. It's easy to begin to feel like you are on your own lonely little island.

I began praying for another Jonathan-David friendship, as I missed this type of friend. The pace of pastoring a growing church and raising four kids was sometimes overwhelming and I just wanted a girlfriend. This may sound funny, but I remember writing an advertisement that I never posted: *Married, pastor's wife and Bible teacher, looking for a best friend. Must love God and be sold out for Him. Must enjoy drinking cappuccinos and cheering for your kids like a wild woman at soccer and basketball games. Sense of humor is a must. To inquire, meet me at Starbucks.*

It wasn't long before the Lord brought Mary into my life. We were like two peas in a pod for a wonderful season. Her friendship was an answer to prayer, a God-knit friendship. I believe God wants to give us those special heart-friends, like Jonathan and David enjoyed.

Jesus had the *multitudes*, the *twelve*, the *three* and the *one* . . . how about you? Why don't you take a sentimental journey and recount the women—the multitudes, the twelve, the three and the one—the Lord has brought in and out of your life?

Friendship Realities

The first thing God said about relationships in the Bible was that it is not good that man should be alone. In other words, it is not good to be lonely. It is not good to be friendless. It is not good to continually fail at relationships.

God wants our relationships to be blessed! Talking, walking, eating, hanging out, playing, praying, working, fighting and serving—the Bible is full of heart-felt, complex, personal and dynamic relationships. God is into people. He is relational. He has created us with a great capacity for friends to give and receive His love to and through others.

Unfortunately, many people—believers and unbelievers alike—are alone. They are lonely. They do not have a heart connection with others. Relationship experts tell us that millions of people in America have never had one minute where they could let down and share their deepest feelings with another person. What about you? Are you one of those people? Are you fulfilled and satisfied in your relationships? Is your heart empty? Lonely? Alone? Is it time to believe God for some friends? Is it time to ask God to blow fresh wind into the sails of your existing friendships?

The Ten Most Wanted Friends

Jesus is our best friend who sticks closer than a brother, He's our first love, but because He knows the value of godly relationships, He brings us together with His family in such a way that He provides divine, God-breathed, God-ordained, God-knit friendships.

God's Word is loaded with wisdom on friendship. God tells us what kind of friend we should be, what type of friend to avoid and how to be a better friend. In their book, *Dealing with People You Can't Stand,* authors Dr. Rick Brinkman and Dr. Rick Kirschner identify the "Ten Most Unwanted" personality types. These are the people you want to avoid and the kind of person you don't want to be. Let's turn that around and see the ten most wanted personality types according to God's Word.

#1. Miss Aromatherapy: A Friend Who Refreshes Our Soul

Candles, lotions, oils, soap, incense and bath beads—you name a scent and you can get it. There is something refreshing about scents and aromas. This is true in friendships, too.

As Christians, we carry the sweet aroma of Christ. *"But thanks be to God! For through what Christ has done, he has triumphed over us so that now wherever we go he uses us to tell others about the Lord and to spread the Gospel like a sweet perfume. As far as God is concerned there is a sweet, wholesome fragrance in our lives. It is the fragrance of Christ within us, an aroma to both the saved and the unsaved all around us. To those who are not being saved, we seem a fearful smell of death and doom, while to those who know Christ we are a life-giving perfume"* (2 Corinthians 2:14-16, TLB).

Let's look at the fragrance of friendship that refreshes us.

1. Proverbs 27:9

   Underline the phrase "sweet friendship."

   > *Just as lotions and fragrance give sensual delight, a sweet friendship refreshes the soul (The Message).*

   Why do you think that lotions and fragrances are compared to a sweet friendship?

   Describe a friend in your life and the type of aroma she gives off.

2. Proverbs 25:13

   Underline the phrase "reliable friends."

   > *Reliable friends who do what they say are like cool drinks in sweltering heat—refreshing! (The Message).*

   What type of friend refreshes us?

   Describe what makes a reliable friend refreshing.

3. 1 Corinthians 16:17-18, 2 Corinthians 7:13

   In these passages, underline the blessings we receive (or give) as friends.

   > *I was glad when Stephanas, Fortunatus and Achaicus arrived, because they have supplied what was lacking from you. For they refreshed my spirit and yours also. Such men deserve recognition (1 Corinthians 16:17-18, NIV).*

   > *By all this we are encouraged. In addition to our own encouragement, we were especially delighted to see how happy Titus was, because his spirit has been refreshed by all of you (2 Corinthians 7:13, NIV).*

   What does getting together with godly friends do for your spirit?

   Describe your get togethers with girlfriends; what type of things do you like to do?

4. Philemon 7

   Underline the words that describe the encouragement Paul received from his Christian friends.

   > *For I have derived great joy and comfort and encouragement from your love, because the hearts of the saints [who are your fellow Christians] have been cheered and refreshed through you, [my] brother (AMP).*

   A godly friend is a gift.

According to this passage, what does a good friend add to our lives?

#2. Miss Lip Balm: A Friend Who Prays

The thing I value most in a friend is her heart to pray. I love to talk, laugh, shop, and hang out with friends, but the thing I most treasure is a friend who prays! A praying friend knows God. To have a praying friend and to be a praying friend is a treasure. When you have a friend who knows how to make real contact with God and pray effectual prayers that heaven answers, you are blessed. If you *are* that type of friend, you are a big blessing!

1. Romans 15:30-32

    Underline the thing that results when we have God-ordained relationships.

    > *Will you be my prayer partners? For the Lord Jesus Christ's sake and because of your love for me—given to you by the Holy Spirit—pray much with me for my work. Pray that I will be protected in Jerusalem from those who are not Christians. Pray also that the Christians there will be willing to accept the money I am bringing them. Then I will be able to come to you with a happy heart by the will of God, and we can refresh each other (TLB).*

    What did Paul need from his friends?

    What types of prayers did Paul request?

What did Paul say would happen for him and his friends when, by God's will, they were united?

2. Job 42:10

Underline the phrase "prayed for his friends."

> *After Job had prayed for his friends, the LORD restored his fortunes and gave him twice as much as he had before (NIV).*

Job's friends had not been that good to Job. Nevertheless, what did Job do for his friends?

What did God end up doing for Job?

If you're looking for help in praying prayers that God will answer, why not pray the prayers that the Holy Spirit inspired Paul to pray for his Christian friends? Just insert your friend's name into these prayers. (If you want to super-size this prayer, I encourage you to read it from the Amplified Bible as well.)

I pray for you (insert your friend's name here) constantly, asking God, the glorious Father of our Lord Jesus Christ, to give you wisdom to see clearly and really understand who Christ is and all that he has done for you. I pray that your hearts will be flooded with light so that you can see something of the future he has called you to share. I want you to realize that God has been made rich because we who are Christ's have been given to him! I pray that you will begin to understand how incredibly great his power is to help those who believe him (Ephesians 1:15-19, TLB).

And I pray that Christ will be more and more at home in your hearts (insert your friend's name here), *living within you as you trust in him. May your roots go down deep into the soil of God's marvelous love; and may you be able to feel and understand, as all God's children should, how long, how wide, how deep, and how high his love really is; and to experience this love for yourselves, though it is so great that you will never see the end of it or fully know or understand it. And so at last you will be filled up with God himself (Ephesians 3:17-18, TLB).*

We have kept on praying and asking God to help you (insert your friend's name here) *understand what he wants you to do; asking him to make you wise about spiritual things; and asking that the way you live will always please the Lord and honor him, so that you will always be doing good, kind things for others, while all the time you are learning to know God better and better. We are praying, too, that you will be filled with his mighty, glorious strength so that you can keep going no matter what happens—always full of the joy of the Lord, and always thankful to the Father who has made us fit to share all the wonderful things that belong to those who live in the Kingdom of light (Colossians 1:9-13, TLB).*

#3. Miss Perfect Bra: A Friend Who Lifts You Up

There is something about finding the right bra—the straps stay in place, it shapes us perfectly, and it gives us the needed lift. In the same way, we need the kind of friends who will lift us up!

John Maxwell describes twenty-five "People Principles" in his book, *Winning with People.* He identifies being the kind of friend who lifts people up, what he calls the Elevator Principle, as one huge key to great relationships. Joyce Landorf Heatherly, author of *Balcony People,* describes the difference between balcony and basement friends. Let's see what the Bible says about friends who lift us up.

1. Exodus 17:12

   Underline the key word that describes Aaron and Hur's help for Moses.

   > *But Moses' hands became heavy; so they took a stone and put it under him, and he sat on it. And Aaron and Hur supported his hands, one on one side, and the other on the other side; and his hands were steady until the going down of the sun (NKJV).*

   What role did Aaron and Hur play in helping Moses get the victory?

   In times of stress, pressure, deadlines, fast-pace, turmoil or emergency, do you have a support system in your life?

   List those who are in your support system:

   Are you the type of person who lifts up those around you?

2. Proverbs 12:25

   Underline one of the causes of depression and one of the causes of gladness.

   > *Anxiety weighs down the heart, but a kind word cheers it up (NIV).*

What does a good word do for us?

Describe a recent experience you've had in hearing a kind word.

Who gave you your last good word?

3. Ephesians 4:29

    Underline the phrase "building others up."

    > *Do not let any unwholesome talk come out of your mouths, but only what is helpful for building others up according to their needs, that it may benefit those who listen (NIV).*

    What type of words should we avoid?

    What type of words should we speak?

    What do good words do for people?

#4. Miss Chocolate Cake: A Friend Who Comforts

Are you a chocoholic? Are there times of the month where you would walk five miles in snow, up a hill both ways, to get chocolate? I know many women who crave chocolate. That's because chocolate is a comfort food. There are times in our lives when we just need some comfort—someone to understand, empathize, encourage and comfort us.

1. Job 2:11-12

    Underline the phrase "Job's three friends."

    > *When Job's three friends, Eliphaz the Temanite, Bildad the Shuhite and Zophar the Naamathite, heard about all the troubles that had come upon him, they set out from their homes and met together by agreement to go and sympathize with him and comfort him (NIV).*

    When Job faced a storm, what did his three friends do?

As it turned out, these friends didn't provide the comfort and wisdom that Job needed. Initially, their hearts were probably in the right place in that they desired to provide comfort. But unfortunately, they did not follow God's wisdom in providing that comfort.

2. 2 Corinthians 7:6

    Underline the things that God did for Paul through his friend, Titus.

    > *But God, Who comforts and encourages and refreshes and cheers the depressed and the sinking, comforted and encouraged and refreshed and cheered us by the arrival of Titus (AMP).*

What did the arrival of Paul's friend, Titus, do for Paul?

It's amazing how the right person at the right time can be used of God to comfort, encourage, refresh and cheer us up.

Who has encouraged you lately?

Who have you encouraged lately?

#5. Miss Double Shot Espresso: A Friend Who Celebrates

Espresso, cappuccino, mochas and lattes, all have the capacity to charge your life with a celebrated burst of energy. If you need an afternoon jolt, what do you drink? Years ago, some of our relatives came to visit our church. They were from a more conservative church background and our style of worship was new and different for them. After church, we asked them how they liked the service. Their comment made us laugh. They said they loved the enthusiastic celebration of worship and described us as "the church on caffeine!" We took that as a compliment. We need those espresso-filled friends in our lives—the energetic, upbeat, positive, motivators—those who will celebrate with us!

It's not always easy to find these types of friends—those who are genuinely happy for our success. Jealousy, envy and competition often enter friendship among women. But it doesn't have to be that way. Who in your life is the "shot in the arm" friend—the one who motivates and celebrates with you? Are you that type of friend?

1. Song of Solomon 5:1

Underline the phrase "Celebrate with me, friends!"

> *Celebrate with me, friends! Raise your glasses—"To life! To love!" (The Message).*

What do we need to do for our friends?

The lover in Song of Solomon wanted her friends to share her joy. It's great to rejoice when good fortune and God's blessings are overflowing in the lives of your friends.

> **NUGGET:** Early in my Christian life, I remember feeling left out, jealous and envious of God's blessings in my friends' lives. That was a sign of my immaturity. All of us have to grow in faith and in God's love, so that we can eliminate jealousy and envy from our lives and rejoice with those who rejoice. There are times when your friend may be celebrating her greatest moments, while you may be facing your most difficult moments. A friend with strong character and an unselfish heart will be able to rejoice in the success and blessing of God in someone else's life, even if their own life does not seem so successful and blessed at the moment. That's when we have to guard against jealousy and envy.

Oprah Winfrey and Gayle King are best friends. I have heard Oprah tell the story of a defining moment in their friendship. When you are in the public eye, you need a friend you can trust. That trust doesn't come easily to someone like Oprah. She's found that friend in Gayle. Oprah says, *"Gayle genuinely—and I could cry when I say this—I have never met a human being more genuinely excited about my success than she is. There has never been one moment of jealousy. I don't know—if our roles were reversed—if I could have given my entire open heart to someone I saw whose career was blast-*

ing off from the earth, and say, 'You go, girl, go to the moon.' I don't know if I could do that."

Describe a time in your life when you overcame the temptation to be jealous or envious of God's blessings in a friend's life.

2. Proverbs 14:10

Underline the phrase "bitter moments" and the word "celebrations."

The person who shuns the bitter moments of friends will be an outsider at their celebrations (The Message).

We need to be the type of friend who is there in the tough times and during the celebrations. We can't just be the "happy" friend; we need to be there with a shoulder to cry on during the tough times, as well.

What does this verse tell us about friendship in bitter moments?

What does this verse tell us about friendship in celebrations?

#6. Miss Double-Dip in a Waffle Cone: A Friend Who is Generous

When the ice cream clerk asks our kids if they want their ice cream in a cup, cone or waffle cone, they turn around and look at us with that *"Pleeeeeeee- ase, can I have a waffle cone"* look. Getting generous scoops of ice cream in a delicious waffle cone is one of life's simple blessings. We need friends like that in our lives and we need to be that type of friend to others, a generous friend.

1. Proverbs 14:20

   Underline the phrase "many friends."

   > *The poor are shunned even by their neighbors, but the rich have many friends (NIV).*

   Who doesn't have friends?

   Who has many friends?

   This verse could be describing a negative truth: because of wrong motives, the rich have lots of friends. Let's think about this verse from the positive side. Since it's true that you cannot give what you do not have, if you were rich in God, rich in joy, rich in peace, rich in wisdom, rich in wealth—and generous in sharing your riches—would people be attracted to you?

   What do you have that you ought to think about giving to others?

2. Proverbs 19:4

   Underline the phrase "attracts friends."

   > *Wealth attracts friends as honey draws flies, but poor people are avoided like a plague (The Message)*

   This passage describes the same thing as Proverbs 14:20.

What does wealth attract?

What does poverty produce?

This is interesting, because as believers we are to reach out to poor and rich alike. God loves people of all economic levels. At the same time, if you have wealth, a humble heart, and are generous with your wealth, you become an attractive friend.

> **NUGGET: Do you think this passage is talking about "buying" friendship? Is it possible to be wealthy in other ways and generous towards your friends and reap real, genuine friendships? In your friendships, are you generous? Are you stingy? Do you always request separate checks when you go to lunch with a friend? Do you offer to buy lunch or mochas? Do you look for ways to give gifts, surprises, notes and other special things to your friends at appropriate and even uneventful times? Be a generous, giving friend!**

3. Isaiah 32:8

   Underline the phrases "generous man," "generous things" and "by generosity."

   > *But a generous man devises generous things, and by generosity he shall stand (NKJV).*

   What does a generous person do?

What makes a person stand and/or stand out?

Have you devised any generous plans lately? Are you on the lookout for ways to be a blessing to your friends? Free yourself from a spirit of stinginess and the next time you go out with your girlfriends, pay the bill and surprise them!

#7. Miss Salt Scrub Exfoliate: A Friend Who Tells You the Truth

These days, there are a plethora of bath and body stores, spas, lotions, ointments, oils, salt scrubs, masks, peels and everybody care product you could want. Those sugar and salt scrubs are great for exfoliating dry, dead skin cells. Do you have people in your life like this? We need exfoliating friends— those who will challenge us, rub us the wrong way at times, and sharpen us! With friends like this, we can be the pure, aromatic and radiant generation of women God has called us to be.

1. Proverbs 2:16

    Underline the phrase "wise friends."

    > *Wise friends will rescue you from the Temptress—that smooth-talking Seductress (The Message).*

    What will a wise and good friend do if she observes you heading down the wrong path?

NUGGET: Don't get mad when your friends tell you the truth. If your girlfriend is heading toward destruction, it takes courage to tell her the truth. I've heard more than one story of women who were unhappy with a friend who told them the truth about a man they were dating. Some women don't want to know the truth about the man they are dating. If you observed your friend making choices that were unhealthy or ungodly, would you have the courage to rescue her by telling her the truth?

2. Proverbs 27:6

Underline the phrase "wounds of a friend."

> *Faithful are the wounds of a friend, but the kisses of an enemy are deceitful (NKJV).*

People who don't love you can flatter you, compliment you, and tell you all the things you want to hear, but in the end what is it?

A true friend tells you the truth, but often what does it feel like?

3. Proverbs 27:17

Underline the phrase "the countenance of his friend."

> *As iron sharpens iron, so a man sharpens the countenance of his friend (NKJV).*

When you rub pieces of iron together, sparks fly, friction heats up, but the iron is sharpened.

How do friends sharpen each other?

How do you handle conflict and disagreement?

In friendship, sometimes there is conflict and disagreement as well as encouragement and accountability.

What does it mean to be accountable to your friends?

When a friend sharpens you, she helps your life become more congruent to God's Word and His will, and the result is a peace and purity that changes your very countenance.

#8. Miss Cosmetic Bag: A Friend Who Covers and Forgives

What's in your make up bag? Foundation, blush, cover up, lipstick, eye shadow, and mascara all serve one purpose—to cover up our imperfections and help us look beautiful. We need friends like that.

1. Proverbs 17:9

    Underline the phrase "close friends."

    Whoever would foster love covers over an offense, but whoever repeats the matter separates close friends (NIV).

    I love how The Message Bible translates this verse.

    Overlook an offense and bond a friendship; fasten on to a slight and—good-bye, friend! (The Message).

If you choose to cover and forgive the sins, offenses, and missteps of your friend, what are you promoting?

How do you cover an offense?

All of us make mistakes. We say the wrong thing, we do the wrong thing, we let our flesh dominate us at times, but it's nice to know we have friends who won't hold our mistakes over our head and blab our faults to others.

If you choose to gossip, criticize, murmur and take offense regarding the faults of your friend, what are you promoting?

We all have imperfections and areas in our lives that need growth. Thank God that as we desire to walk in the light of His Word and please Him, He is patient and kind towards us. He's merciful and forgiving. We need to give that same type of love, mercy and forgiveness to our friends.

2. Colossians 3:13

Underline the words "forgive" and "forgave."

Make allowance for each other's faults and forgive anyone who offends you. Remember, the Lord forgave you, so you must forgive others (NLT).

What are we supposed to remember?

What are we supposed to make allowances for?

Who are we to forgive?

#9. Miss Outdoor Café: A Friend Who Shares Your Love for God

Talking with friends about the Lord, His Word, and life in general is a real blessing. Let's look at those types of friends.

1. Malachi 3:16

    Underline the phrase "lives honored God."

    > *Then those whose lives honored GOD got together and talked it over. GOD saw what they were doing and listened in. A book was opened in God's presence and minutes were taken of the meeting, with the names of the GOD—fearers written down, all the names of those who honored GOD's name (The Message).*

    What did these Christian friends do?

    Who was listening to their conversation?

What did God do?

Describe the last "God-talk" you had with one of your friends.

NUGGET: God recorded it! Isn't that a great thought? I can just imagine an entire wing of God's massive, heavenly library filled with "Conversation Books." So, let's give Him something to write about! The next time you and your girlfriends get together, take the initiative to move the conversation toward the things of God. Ask interesting questions to hear what He is doing in their lives.

2.   2 Timothy 1:16-18

Underline the phrases that describe the way Onesiphorus encouraged Paul in the Lord.

> *The Lord grant mercy to the household of Onesiphorus, for he often refreshed me, and was not ashamed of my chain; but when he arrived in Rome, he sought me out very zealously and found me. The Lord grant to him that he may find mercy from the Lord in that Day—and you know very well how many ways he ministered to me at Ephesus (NKJV).*

Onesiphorus knew of Paul's suffering in ministry and perhaps he thought Paul might be discouraged, so he took the initiative to find and encourage Paul. He ministered to Paul. As Paul was refreshed, he could continue to preach the gospel. Onesiphorus must have kept tabs on Paul's life and ministry—perhaps he was a prayer warrior, a ministry partner, or just a dear friend. In any event, he was a blessing to Paul.

Describe the role of taking the initiative in friendship.

What did Onesiphorus do for Paul?

Sometimes as we share Christ with others, we face persecution from our families, friends or co-workers. That's when it's nice to have a friend to root us on in the Lord. It's a blessing to have a friend who loves God and shares the same passion as we do for the gospel.

3. Psalm 16:3

    Underline the phrase "my true heroes."

    > *The godly people in the land are my true heroes! I take plea-sure in them (NLT).*

    Listen to how the Message Bible puts it . . .

    > *And these God-chosen lives all around—what splendid friends they make (The Message).*

    What type of friends are your heroes?

NUGGET: Think about your circle of friends. Do you have a strong group of Christian friends you can relate to? On one hand, we are all in the family of God and we ought to love and relate easily to everyone in the Body of Christ, regardless of common interests. Yet, at the same time, we all seek to find or belong to a small group or circle of friends in which we share similar interests. I have found that often in the church world, people can come and go and never really find "their people." For some reason, it seems that because of insecurities or false ideas, we assume that others are not interested in us. We think they are more spiritual, smarter, richer, or more together then we are, therefore they certainly wouldn't want to be our friend. That is a lie and it has robbed people of rich friendships. It's true that all of us relate to different kinds of people. Generally, when a person enters a crowded room, church service, party or social setting, they immediately scan the room to find "their people." In other words, we often look for people in our general age range and similar season of life. We try to find those whom we have something in common. In the church world, when people don't find "their people" immediately, they often quit looking. Eventually, they fade away from fellowshipping with Christians and serving the Lord in their community.

I encourage you to be proactive in seeking Christian friends. Make it a point to attend events where potential friendships would be—church services, small groups, Bible studies, women's events and other environments where God can connect you to other dynamic Christian gals. The Lord wants all of us to have deep, heartfelt friendships with other believers—people who share our love for God. It's needed. It's healthy and we should cultivate and take pleasure in the godly friends God has put in our lives.

#10.   Miss Pantyhose: A Friend Who Sticks with You

Pantyhose have a way of sticking to us. We need friends who will stick with us through thick or thin.

1.   Proverbs 17:17

Underline the phrase "friends love."

Friends love through all kinds of weather, and families stick together in all kinds of trouble (The Message).

When do friends love us?

Don't be a fair weather friend; stick it out through every season. There inevitably are seasons and transitions in friendship, but be the type of friend who doesn't bail when the chips are down.

2. Proverbs 18:24

Underline the phrase "a true friend."

Friends come and friends go, but a true friend sticks by you like family (The Message).

What's the difference between a "friend" and a "true friend"?

Make a list of your friends.

Make a list of your "true" friends.

Scriptures to Meditate On

Just as lotions and fragrance give sensual delight,
a sweet friendship refreshes the soul.

Proverbs 27:9, The Message

Then those whose lives honored GOD got together and talked it over.
GOD saw what they were doing and listened in.
A book was opened in God's presence and minutes were taken
of the meeting, with the names of the GOD-fearers written down,
all the names of those who honored GOD's name.

Malachi 3:16, The Message

Group Discussion

1. In the "Ten Most Wanted" friends, which three traits do you desire most in the friends in your life? Why?

2. In the "Ten Most Wanted" friends, which three traits do you need to improve on the most? Why?

3. Describe the blessing of having a friend who shares your love for God. Can you describe a season where you did not have this type of friend? Share the way you found this type of friend.

CHAPTER 2
The Friendship Workout

Maybe you are wondering, *How? How can I be a better friend? How can I start sowing some friend seeds? How can I improve my current friendships?* If you're feeling like a flabby friend, it's time to hit God's Gym and work the friendship building workout stations circuit. Let's look at what the Bible says about a friendship workout—guaranteed to define and build your friendship muscles.

The 12 "One Another" Stations

In order to make this work as a regular part of your life, it is going to require two big paradigm changes. Are you ready?

First, it's your attitude. You will have to shift from the "Here I am" perspective to the "There you are" approach. That means in all of your relational dealings, it's not about you—it's about them. Your focus isn't on how you look, sound or appear, or on what you are going to say, share or do, but rather on the person or people you are with and how you can enrich their lives by practically incorporating the "One Another" workout into your relational life.

Listen to this encouragement: *"Is there any such thing as Christians cheering each other up? Do you love me enough to want to help me? Does it mean anything to you that we are brothers in the Lord, sharing the same Spirit? Are your hearts tender and sympathetic at all? Then make me truly happy by loving each other and agreeing wholeheartedly with each other, working together with one heart and mind and purpose. Don't be selfish; don't live to make a good impression on others. Be humble, thinking of others as better than yourself. Don't just think about your own affairs, but be interested in*

others, too, and in what they are doing" (Philippians 2:1-4, TLB). Here's another one: *"Let no one seek his own, but each one the other's well-being"*
(1 Corinthians 10:24, NKJV).

Second, you've got to get dressed. Here's the designer workout outfit: *"So,*
chosen by God for this new life of love, dress in the wardrobe God picked
out for you: compassion, kindness, humility, quiet strength, discipline. Be
even-tempered, content with second place, quick to forgive an offense. For-
give as quickly and completely as the Master forgave you. And regardless of
what else you put on, wear love. It's your basic, all-purpose garment. Never
be without it" (Colossians 3:12-14, The Message).

Okay, now that our attitudes are changed and we're dressed, let's hit God's
gym and work it out.

Station #1: Love One Another

This is the most important station. Let's look at several verses of Scripture in
the New Testament to see how many times this is reiterated.

1. John 13:34, 15:12, 15:17

    Underline the phrase "love one another."

    > *A new commandment I give unto you, That ye love one an-*
    > *other; as I have loved you, that ye also love one another (John*
    > *13:34, KJV).*

    > *This is my commandment, That ye love one another, as I have*
    > *loved you (John 15:12, KJV).*

    > *These things I command you, that ye love one another (John*
    > *15:17, KJV).*

What is Jesus' new commandment for New Testament believers?

How are we to love one another?

The good news under the New Testament is that we only have to keep one command, rather than thousands of commandments. The one command is to love!

2. Romans 13:8

    Underline the phrase "love one another."

    Owe no man any thing, but to love one another: for he that loveth another hath fulfilled the law (KJV).

    If we want to fulfill all of God's requirements under the Old Testament Law, what must we do?

3. 1 Thessalonians 4:9

    Underline the phrase "love one another."

    But as touching brotherly love ye need not that I write unto you: for ye yourselves are taught of God to love one another (KJV).

    Who teaches us to love one another?

CLICK

What are some practical ways to love others?

4. 1 John 3:11, 23 and 4:7-12

Underline the phrase "love one another."

> *For this is the message that ye heard from the beginning, that we should love one another (1 John 3:11, KJV).*

> *And this is his commandment, That we should believe on the name of his Son Jesus Christ, and love one another, as he gave us commandment (1 John 3:23, KJV).*

> *Beloved, let us love one another: for love is of God; and every one that loveth is born of God, and knoweth God. He that loveth not knoweth not God; for God is love. In this was manifested the love of God toward us, because that God sent his only begotten Son into the world, that we might live through him. Herein is love, not that we loved God, but that he loved us, and sent his Son to be the propitiation for our sins. Beloved, if God so loved us, we ought also to love one another. No man hath seen God at any time. If we love one another, God dwelleth in us, and his love is perfected in us (1 John 4:7-12, KJV).*

Where does love originate?

Who loved first?

If God loved us, how does that enable us to love others?

In practical terms, how can we love one another?

5. 1 Peter 1:22

Underline the phrase "love one another."

> *Seeing ye have purified your souls in obeying the truth through the Spirit unto unfeigned love of the brethren, see that ye love one another with a pure heart fervently (KJV).*

According to this passage, how are we to love one another?

6. 2 John 1:5

Underline the phrase "love one another."

> *And now I beseech thee, lady, not as though I wrote a new commandment unto thee, but that which we had from the beginning, that we love one another (KJV).*

One more time, what is the new commandment?

Get the idea? Over and over, Jesus and the writers of the New Testament emphasized the importance of loving God and loving one another as Jesus loves us. This is the command that we are to obey as New Testament believers. We don't have to remember the Ten Commandments nor do we have to remember the hundreds of Old Testament laws; we only have to remember the New Commandment which is summed up as loving God and loving others. It's easy to remember, but it will take our entire spirit, soul and body to obey.

Station #2: Be Devoted to One Another

1. Romans 12:10

   Underline the phrase "be devoted to one another."

   Be devoted to one another in love (NIV).

   How would you define "devoted"?

2. 1 Corinthians 16:15

   Underline the phrase "devoted themselves."

   I urge you, brethren—you know the household of Stephanas, that it is the firstfruits of Achaia, and that they have devoted themselves to the ministry of the saints (NKJV).

   To what did this family devote themselves?

Station #3: Accept One Another

1. Romans 15:7

   Underline the phrase "accept one another."

Accept one another, then, just as Christ accepted you, in order to bring praise to God (NIV).

How should we accept one another?

Describe this in real life.

2. Romans 14:13

Underline the phrase "judge one another."

Let us not therefore judge one another any more (KJV).

What are we not to do to one another?

NUGGET: When we choose to accept one another, flaws and all, we are walking in God's love. To accept one another does not necessarily mean that we condone all behavior. There are certain personalities that rub us the wrong way. People have idiosyncrasies that can seem odd. There may be some people whom you don't "like" per se, but we are commanded to love and accept one another.

Describe a scenario in which you've had to accept someone you didn't particularly like or someone who rubbed you the wrong way.

Station #4: Instruct One Another

1. Romans 15:14

   Underline the phrase "instruct one another."

   > *I myself am convinced, my brothers and sisters, that you yourselves are full of goodness, filled with knowledge and competent to instruct one another (NIV).*

   According to this verse, what makes a person competent to instruct others?

2. Colossians 3:16

   Underline the phrase "instruct and direct one another."

   > *Let the Word of Christ—the Message—have the run of the house. Give it plenty of room in your lives. Instruct and direct one another using good common sense. And sing, sing your hearts out to God (The Message).*

   According to this verse, what gives us the ability to instruct and direct one another?

NUGGET: If we are humble and teachable, we can learn from just about anyone. I love learning from others and hearing the things the Lord has shared with them. Any time someone sheds new light on the Scriptures or shares a nugget of truth from the Word, I am blessed. Talking to and sharing with our friends is great, but very few people appreciate being preached to if it is not solicited.

Station #5: Serve One Another

1. Galatians 5:13-14

   Underline the phrase "serve one another."

   > *You, my brothers and sisters, were called to be free. But do not use your freedom to indulge the flesh; rather, serve one another humbly in love. The entire law is fulfilled in keeping this one command: "Love your neighbor as yourself" (NIV).*

   Who in your life could you do a better job serving?

   In what ways can we serve one another?

   NUGGET: Serving others is love in action. Acts of service is the love language of some people, according to Gary Chapman in his book *The Five Love Languages*.[1] Making meals, cleaning the home, washing the car, doing the laundry, serving a cup of coffee, carrying the luggage, making breakfast in bed, and other gestures of service come easily and naturally for those who find acts of service their primary love language. The rest of us really have to be on the lookout for the needs around us and ways to serve others.

2. 1 Peter 4:10

   Underline the phrase "serve others."

   > *Each of you should use whatever gift you have received to serve others, as faithful stewards of God's grace in its various forms (NIV).*

---

1 Chapman, Gary D. *The Five Love Languages*. Chicago: Moody Publishers, 1996. (pg 59)

What gifts and talents has God graced you with and how are you using them to serve others?

Station #6: Bear with One Another

1. Ephesians 4:1-2

Underline the phrase "bearing with one another."

Be completely humble and gentle; be patient, bearing with one another in love (NIV).

What do you think it means to "bear" with others?

NUGGET: The word "bearing" in the King James Bible is the word "forbearing," and according to Strong's Concordance this means "to hold oneself up against." Figuratively it means to put up with. It's also translated to mean "bear with, endure and suffer."[2] Have you ever had to bear with someone while they went through a difficult time, grief or some transition or dramatic life change? Have you ever had to put up with someone at a family reunion, office party or neighborhood barbecue? Ever had to bear with someone during their time of weakness, repentance and the recovery process? Have you had to endure a certain person's personality or quirks, or patiently supported and suffered through things with an individual? If so, you were bearing with one another in love!

---

2 *Biblesoft's New Exhaustive Strong's Numbers and Concordance with Expanded Greek-Hebrew Dictionary.* Copyright © 1994, 2003 Biblesoft, Inc. and International Bible Translators, Inc.

2. Colossians 3:13

Underline the phrase "bear with each other."

> *Bear with each other and forgive one another if any of you has a grievance against someone. Forgive as the Lord forgave you (NIV).*

What other act of love seems to accompany bearing with one another?

Often as we put up with people, we find that we have to extend a lot of forgiveness and grace. Do you have people in your life whom you just have to endure and put up with? If so, how will you be better at bearing with them?

Station #7: Be Affectionate with One Another

1. 1 Peter 5:14

Underline the phrase "salute one another with a kiss."

> *Salute one another with a kiss of love [the symbol of mutual affection] (AMP).*

How would you describe this display of affection?

Are there times when "a kiss of love" would not be appropriate? If so, when?

In what ways can you extend Christlike affection to those around you in appropriate ways without being uncomfortably "touchy" or "ice cold"?

In some cultures, kissing others is quite common. Men kiss men on both sides of the cheek as do the women. In other cultures, friends will greet one another with a handshake, hug or embrace. In the church world, we've seen some people who are "huggy and kissy" to everyone they meet, but for some folks this is quite uncomfortable. We've also seen other folks who were so stiff and stoic, you didn't know if they loved you or hated you. God wants us to greet one another with brotherly love in an authentic and affectionate way.

2. 1 Thessalonians 2:8

Underline the phrase "an affection for you."

> *Having so fond an affection for you, we were well-pleased to impart to you not only the gospel of God but also our own lives, because you had become very dear to us (NASB).*

Having affection for others will lead us to impart what two things?

Station #8: Be Kind to One Another

1. Ephesians 4:32

Underline the phrase "kind one to another."

> *And be ye kind one to another, tenderhearted (KJV).*

How would you define kind and tenderhearted?

2. 1 Corinthians 13:4

Underline the phrase "love is kind."

> *Love is patient, love is kind. It does not envy, it does not boast, it is not proud (NIV).*

Love is what?

Love does not do what?

Station #9: Be Forgiving to One Another

1. Ephesians 4:32

Underline the phrase "forgiving one another."

> *Forgiving one another, even as God for Christ's sake hath forgiven you (KJV).*

Have you ever needed forgiveness?

Has God forgiven you?

CLICK

How are we to forgive one another?

Can you hold a grudge or unforgiveness against anyone when Jesus has forgiven you of all your sins?

Jesus told us to forgive anyone of anything. If we ever think we have the right to withhold forgiveness from anyone for anything, we need to reread Mark 11:25-26, pronto!

2. Colossians 3:13

    Underline the words "forgive whatever" and "against one another."

    Forgive one another. If any of you has a grievance against someone. Forgive as the Lord forgave you (NIV).

    According to this verse, what grievances are you allowed to maintain?

Station #10: Comfort One Another

1. 1 Thessalonians 4:18

    Underline the phrase "comfort one another."

    Wherefore comfort one another with these words (KJV).

    What can we comfort others with?

In this passage, the Apostle Paul was specifically telling us that we can comfort one another with words about Jesus' second coming and our eternal destiny with Jesus. Other passages in the Bible, particularly in Proverbs, tell us that our words can literally comfort and minister grace and pleasantness to the hearer. Use your mouth to comfort others!

2. 1 Thessalonians 5:11

    Underline the phrase "comfort yourselves" and "edify one another."

    Wherefore comfort yourselves together, and edify one another, even as also ye do (KJV).

    How can we comfort and edify one another?

Again, one way we can give comfort and edification is through our words. Read Ephesians 4:29 for a great description of the power of our words.

Station #11: Exhort One Another

1. Hebrews 3:13

    Underline the phrase "exhort one another."

    But exhort one another daily, while it is called To day; lest any of you be hardened through the deceitfulness of sin (KJV).

    How often should we exhort others?

Why is it necessary to be exhorted?

How would you define "exhort"?

NUGGET: Exhort is from the Greek word "parakaleoo." Its meaning includes "to admonish, to beg, entreat, beseech, console, encourage, comfort and strengthen by consolation."[3]

2. Hebrews 10:24-25

Underline the phrases "consider one another" and "exhorting one another."

> *And let us consider one another to provoke unto love and to good works: Not forsaking the assembling of ourselves together, as the manner of some is; but exhorting one another: and so much the more, as ye see the day approaching (KJV).*

What are we to provoke one another to do?

What are we to encourage people not to forsake?

Describe the intensity and frequency with which we should be exhorting one another.

---

3 From *Thayer's Greek Lexicon,* Electronic Database. Copyright © 2000, 2003 by Biblesoft, Inc. All rights reserved.

NUGGET: One of the enemy's most effective snares is to convince, distract and turn people from going to church where they will gather with other believers for worship, the Word, and strength for their God-given assignments. Often the greatest challenges people fall into are busyness and apathy. They get busy with their jobs, sports and leisure and begin to fall into the trap of thinking, Sunday is our only day off and we want to spend it with our kids, doing yard work, sleeping, watching TV and football games, reading, counting the carpet fibers in our family room, watching the grass grow, or you will hear people make comments like, "I don't need church, God can talk to me and my family at home just fine. I connect with God better when I am enjoying God's creation—fishing, skiing, boating, cleaning, painting, sleeping, digging a hole to China," and so on. This is a slippery slope to snuffing out our spiritual light.

As one preacher said, "When you have a bonfire, all the logs glow brightly and stay ablaze, but when you pull one log off the fire and set it aside, it's just a matter of time until the log loses its fire." It's the same way with our faith. When we are regularly attending church, worshipping God, growing in the Word and reaching out to others, we stay aglow with God's Spirit. But when we quit attending church, our flame begins to go out and grow cold like the lone log.

We need to be exhorted and we need to exhort others to get into church on a regular basis. If we are drying up on the vine, spiritually speaking, we need to stir ourselves up and be diligent to attend a good Bible preaching church.

Station #12: Honor One Another

1. Romans 12:10

    Underline the phrase "honor one another."

    Honor one another above yourselves (NIV).

How should we honor others?

In your own words, how do you define honor?

NUGGET: The Greek word for honor is time, and its meaning includes a value, esteem, precious.[4]

In what ways can you honor others?

NUGGET: We live in a casual society, and in some ways that has been a good thing. But in other ways, our casual attitude has translated into disrespect and dishonor toward others. When we were kids, we were taught to address adults by Mr. and Mrs., to respect authority, and to honor the office a person holds. Today, kids call adults by their first names, authority has been dismissed, and people don't know the spiritual implications of honoring the office of the President, the police, their boss, teacher or pastor. When we esteem others as valuable and precious and validate that with our actions, we are showing honor.

2. Galatians 5:26

    Underline these words: "vainglorious," "self-conceited," "competitive," "challenging," "provoking," "irritating," "envying" and "jealous."

    Let us not become vainglorious and self-conceited, competitive and challenging and provoking and irritating to one another, envying and being jealous of one another (AMP).

---

4 Strong's.

What should we avoid?

In your friendships, where do you need to improve?

Scriptures to Meditate On

Let no one seek his own, but each one the other's well-being.

1 Corinthians 10:24, NKJV

Beloved, let us love one another: for love is of God;
and every one that loveth is born of God, and knoweth God.
He that loveth not knoweth not God; for God is love.

1 John 4:7-8, KJV

Group Discussion

1. Describe the way you can become a "There you are" type of friend, more than a "Here I am" type of friend.

2. Which of the 12 "One Another" stations do you need to spend more time working on?

3. Which one of the 12 "One Another" stations is the biggest challenge for you?

CHAPTER 3
God-Knit Friendships

Smart friends. Kindred spirit. God-knit. God-breathed friendships. Been praying for a friend? Looking for a bosom buddy? A best friend?

Remember Anne of Green Gables? She wondered:

". . . do you think that I shall ever have a bosom friend . . . ?"

"A—a what kind of friend?"

"A bosom friend—an intimate friend, you know—a really kindred spirit to whom I can confide my inmost soul. I've dreamed of meeting her all my life. I never really supposed I would, but so many of my loveliest dreams have come true all at once that perhaps this one will, too. Do you think it's possible?"[5]

Yes, it's possible! Jesus had this type of relationship. Jonathan and David enjoyed this type of friendship. I believe these are special, God-ordained types of friendships—God-knit, God-breathed. If you are married, it's likely that your husband is your best friend and soul mate, and perhaps you also have a nice circle of gal friends to hang out with. Yet at the same time, I know many women who long for a close girl friend and confidant. I've been blessed with three girl friendships, "bosom friends" or Jonathan-David type friendships in my life and in each case, God knit our hearts together in such a way that we were almost closer than blood sisters. These friendships are priceless treasures!

Jesus enjoyed relationships on all levels: with the multitudes, the twelve disciples, the three (Peter, James and John) and the one (John). We see Jesus

---

5 *Anne of Green Gables.* Montgomery L. M. Public Domain, 1908.

minister to the *multitudes* in healing, feeding, preaching and teaching. Then we see Him pour into His *twelve* disciples; He took the *three*—Peter, James and John—with Him to the mount of transfiguration. Then we watch the *one* apostle, John, lay his head on Jesus' chest at the Last Supper.

> NUGGET: It seems God always has a greater purpose for these types of friendships. One minister has said it this way: "God always leads us to people who will lead us to Him." The Lord often uses Jonathan-David type friendships to help propel us further in our walk with Him—our prayer life and His plan, purpose and destiny for our lives. He gives us these friends to walk through various seasons of life: college, work, marriage, child-rearing, or menopause—the ebb and flow of life. It's nice to have a heart friend to call when you need a favor or help with your kids, when you need prayer or a shoulder to cry on, when you need a spiritual kick in the pants, or when you just need someone to help you paint your kitchen or pray for your husband's new job. In any case, it's a blessing to have a God-breathed friendship. Have you considered His purposes in your friendships? What season of life are you in and how does He want your friendship to add value to your life and theirs? Does He want to lead you into a new place of prayer? Increase your hunger for the Word? Prepare you for ministry or give you a heart for the lost? God uses this type of friendship to lead us to a more mature place in Him.

Do you desire a God-friend like this? I've talked with lots of women over the years and the universal cry I hear is the longing gals have for a "best friend." They love their husbands dearly, but they desire the friendship that other women add to their lives. A prayer partner. A confidant. Most people have acquaintances and co-workers they can chum with, but few women have one or two unique, heart friends they can confide in.

I believe God wants to answer your desire for a friend and as you study this chapter, I pray that you receive His wisdom on discovering and cultivating a Jonathan-David friendship. Let's look at the dynamics of a God-breathed friendship, like the one that Jonathan and David enjoyed, to see what insights we can glean.

Divine Clickage

1. 1 Samuel 18:1-4

    Underline the phrases "Jonathan became one in spirit with David," and "he loved him as himself."

    > *After David had finished talking with Saul, Jonathan became one in spirit with David, and he loved him as himself. From that day Saul kept David with him and did not let him return home to his family. And Jonathan made a covenant with David because he loved him as himself. Jonathan took off the robe he was wearing and gave it to David, along with his tunic, and even his sword, his bow and his belt (NIV).*

    What caused Jonathan to become one in spirit with David?

    How does this passage describe the love that Jonathan had in his heart for David?

During this encounter while David was chatting with Jonathan's dad, God put something in Jonathan's heart which initiated what I call "friendship clickage." It seems that God put His love in Jonathan's heart for David. Perhaps when Jonathan heard David speaking, he liked his personality, his heart for God or his sense of humor, and God put a love for David inside Jonathan's heart. Sometimes we say when there is clickage that God connects you supernaturally and it's as if you've found your people. It's a God-thing!

NUGGET: As we've mentioned, God always leads us to people who will lead us to Him. In light of God's call on David to be king of Israel and in light of the difficulties that David was about to face, is it possible that God knit Jonathan's soul to David to be a source of rich and much needed encouragement, wisdom and help? At the same time, we'll see that God knew Jonathan's future as well, and because of the covenant of their friendship, David's love for Jonathan precipitated his care for Jonathan's family. It seems that these Jonathan-David type friendships often have a divine purpose in mutually propelling us into God's will. God knows our future and His calling and purpose, and He brings friends into our lives who help encourage, refresh, protect and motivate us to fulfill our destiny.

Think about it. Are you praying for a God-breathed friend? It's very possible that God has already put this friend in your life and that they are also praying for a Jonathan-David type friend. God's Word says that He knows what we need before we ask Him. He orders our steps and provides everything we need in order to fulfill His will in our lives—including rich friendships.

Has God put anyone in your life you find you gravitate toward or just seem to click with? Do you sense God's unconditional love in your heart for someone in your life? Often, if we can locate God's love on the inside of us and then follow His love, it will lead us to people He wants to connect us with. I have found that in each of the God-breathed friendships the Lord has given me, He put a divine "click" in my heart.

NUGGET: One little caveat . . . relationships and particularly "Jonathan-David Friendships" require a mutual, God-given desire for friendship. At times, God will drop His love in your heart for a particular person not because He wants you to become their friend, but simply because He wants you to pray for them or encourage them. He gives you a snippet of His love and as you follow His love, it will lead you to pray for, lift up and encourage those God puts in your heart.

For example, there have been several occasions where the Lord has put His love for someone in my heart and I felt great compassion for them. I have learned to identify that this love was in my heart simply so I could pray for that person in a particular season of their life, but a friendship with them was not in God's plan. His love in my heart was there purely to motivate me to pray for them.

On the other hand, at times, God will put His love for someone in your heart and at the same time, He will put His love for you in their heart. There is a mutual sense of "divine clickage" and both parties will have a desire to develop a friendship. If God has put someone in your heart but you are not in their heart, don't force it, don't be upset, and don't be discouraged. God is the one who gives people a place in our hearts and God is the one who will give you a place in others' hearts. If you want to enjoy His divine plan for friendship, the most important thing you can do is identify who God has put in your heart and then follow His love to be a blessing to them. If He has put you in their heart, they will likely automatically reciprocate and a friendship will begin to blossom.

Have you experienced this type of friendship where there was a mutual divine click and a God-breathed friendship developed? If so, describe it.

Have you experienced God's love in your heart for someone for the purpose of motivating you to pray for them?

2. 1 Samuel 19:1-3, 6-7

Underline the phrase "Jonathan was very fond of David."

Saul told his son Jonathan and all the attendants to kill David. But Jonathan had taken a great liking to David and warned

*him, "My father Saul is looking for a chance to kill you. Be on
your guard tomorrow morning; go into hiding and stay there.
I will go out and stand with my father in the field where you
are. I'll speak to him about you and will tell you what I find
out" (1 Samuel 19:1-3, NIV).*

*Saul listened to Jonathan and took this oath: "As surely as
the LORD lives, David will not be put to death." So Jonathan
called David and told him the whole conversation. He brought
him to Saul, and David was with Saul as before (1 Samuel
19:6-7, NIV).*

I love how the New King James Version brings out 1 Samuel 19:1.

*Now Saul spoke to Jonathan his son and to all his servants,
that they should kill David; but Jonathan, Saul's son, delighted greatly in David (NKJV).*

How does verse 1 describe Jonathan's heart toward David?

**NUGGET: Notice that God-ordained friendships are delightful. We've
all experienced relationships that are draining, high maintenance
and a lot of work. It's wonderful to find friends who refresh and delight your heart and bring you joy. All relationships take work, but
there are certain friendships that tend to be more draining than
refreshing. When God knits your heart together in a "Jonathan-David" type of friendship, there is a sense of delight that tends to
energize and refresh you, rather than drain and sap you. You look
forward to getting together, rather than dreading it!**

In verse 1, Jonathan's father Saul had become very jealous of David's success and wanted to kill him. It's obvious that Jonathan's friendship with David
superseded the relationship Jonathan had with his own father.

58

Because of his love for David, what did Jonathan do for David? Jonathan was fond of David and he worked hard to protect David from his own father's evil agenda.

Divine Commitment

1. 1 Samuel 20:1-42

    Underline the phrases "I have found favor in your eyes," "Whatever you want me to do, I'll do for you," "he loved him as he loved himself" and "we have sworn friendship with each other in the name of the LORD."

    Then David fled from Naioth at Ramah and went to Jonathan and asked, "What have I done? What is my crime? How have I wronged your father, that he is trying to kill me?"

    "Never!" Jonathan replied. "You are not going to die! Look, my father doesn't do anything, great or small, without letting me know. Why would he hide this from me? It isn't so!"

    But David took an oath and said, "Your father knows very well that I have found favor in your eyes, and he has said to himself, 'Jonathan must not know this or he will be grieved.' Yet as surely as the LORD lives and as you live, there is only a step between me and death."

    Jonathan said to David, "Whatever you want me to do, I'll do for you."

    So David said, "Look, tomorrow is the New Moon feast, and I am supposed to dine with the king; but let me go and hide in the field until the evening of the day after tomorrow. If your father misses me at all, tell him, 'David earnestly asked my permission to hurry to Bethlehem, his hometown, because an annual sacrifice is being made there for his whole clan.' If he says, 'Very well,' then your servant is safe. But if he loses his temper, you can be sure that he is determined to harm me. As for you, show kindness to your servant, for you have brought him into a covenant with you before the LORD. If I am guilty, then kill me yourself! Why hand me over to your father?"

"Never!" Jonathan said. "If I had the least inkling that my father was determined to harm you, wouldn't I tell you?"

David asked, "Who will tell me if your father answers you harshly?"

"Come," Jonathan said, "let's go out into the field." So they went there together.

Then Jonathan said to David, "I swear by the LORD, the God of Israel, that I will surely sound out my father by this time the day after tomorrow! If he is favorably disposed toward you, will I not send you word and let you know? But if my father intends to harm you, may the LORD deal with Jonathan, be it ever so severely, if I do not let you know and send you away in peace. May the LORD be with you as he has been with my father. But show me unfailing kindness like the LORD'S kindness as long as I live, so that I may not be killed, and do not ever cut off your kindness from my family—not even when the LORD has cut off every one of David's enemies from the face of the earth."

So Jonathan made a covenant with the house of David, saying, "May the LORD call David's enemies to account." And Jonathan had David reaffirm his oath out of love for him, because he loved him as he loved himself.

Then Jonathan said to David, "Tomorrow is the New Moon feast. You will be missed, because your seat will be emp-

ty. The day after tomorrow, toward evening, go to the place where you hid when this trouble began, and wait by the stone Ezel. I will shoot three arrows to the side of it, as though I were shooting at a target. Then I will send a boy and say, 'Go, find the arrows.' If I say to him, 'Look, the arrows are on this side of you; bring them here,' then come, because, as surely as the LORD lives, you are safe; there is no danger. But if I say to the boy, 'Look, the arrows are beyond you,' then you must go, because the LORD has sent you away. And about the matter you and I discussed—remember, the LORD is witness between you and me forever."

So David hid in the field, and when the New Moon feast came, the king sat down to eat. He sat in his customary place by the wall, opposite Jonathan, and Abner sat next to Saul, but David's place was empty. Saul said nothing that day, for he thought, "Something must have happened to David to make him ceremonially unclean—surely he is unclean." But the next day, the second day of the month, David's place was empty again. Then Saul said to his son Jonathan, "Why hasn't the son of Jesse come to the meal, either yesterday or today?"

Jonathan answered, "David earnestly asked me for permission to go to Bethlehem. He said, 'Let me go, because our family is observing a sacrifice in the town and my brother has ordered me to be there. If I have found favor in your eyes, let me get away to see my brothers.' That is why he has not come to the king's table."

Saul's anger flared up at Jonathan and he said to him, "You son of a perverse and rebellious woman! Don't I know that you have sided with the son of Jesse to your own shame and to the shame of the mother who bore you? As long as the son of Jesse lives on this earth, neither you nor your kingdom will be established. Now send someone to bring him to me, for he must die!"

"Why should he be put to death? What has he done?" Jonathan asked his father. But Saul hurled his spear at him to kill him. Then Jonathan knew that his father intended to kill David.

Jonathan got up from the table in fierce anger; on that second day of the feast he did not eat, because he was grieved at his father's shameful treatment of David.

In the morning Jonathan went out to the field for his meeting with David. He had a small boy with him, and he said to the boy, "Run and find the arrows I shoot." As the boy ran, he shot an arrow beyond him. When the boy came to the place where Jonathan's arrow had fallen, Jonathan called out after him, "Isn't the arrow beyond you?" Then he shouted, "Hurry! Go quickly! Don't stop!" The boy picked up the arrow and returned to his master. (The boy knew nothing about all this; only Jonathan and David knew.) Then Jonathan gave his weapons to the boy and said, "Go, carry them back to town."

After the boy had gone, David got up from the south side of the stone and bowed down before Jonathan three times, with his face to the ground. Then they kissed each other and wept together—but David wept the most.

Jonathan said to David, "Go in peace, for we have sworn friendship with each other in the name of the LORD, saying, 'The LORD is witness between you and me, and between your descendants and my descendants forever.'" Then David left, and Jonathan went back to the town (NIV).

Why did Saul want to kill David? (vs 1, 30-33)

In verses 2, 4, 12, 16-17, 23, 28-29, 32-33, 35, 40-42, what was Jonathan's commitment to David?

In verse 4, 16-17, 41-42, we get a picture of the heartfelt love that Jonathan and David had for one another.

Describe how Jonathan felt about David.

Describe how David felt about Jonathan.

Notice how vulnerable David and Jonathan were and how freely they communicated their affection and commitment to love and bless one another and their families.

NUGGET: One secret to lasting, heartfelt, rich relationships is a commitment to communicate. This includes being vulnerable, being interested, being honest and being transparent. It's impossible to have a strong relationship with anyone without a deep level of communication that goes beyond the casual, surface conversation. Communication requires risk. Are you willing to commit yourself to honest communication?

2. 1 Samuel 23:15-18

Underline the phrase "The two of them made a covenant before the LORD."

> *While David was at Horesh in the Desert of Ziph, he learned*
> *that Saul had come out to take his life. And Saul's son Jon-*
> *athan went to David at Horesh and helped him find strength*
> *in God. "Don't be afraid," he said. "My father Saul will not*
> *lay a hand on you. You will be king over Israel, and I will be*
> *second to you. Even my father Saul knows this." The two of*
> *them made a covenant before the LORD. Then Jonathan went*
> *home, but David remained at Horesh (NIV).*

In what way did Jonathan continue to encourage David?

What type of covenant did Jonathan and David make? They had agreed that the Lord would watch between them and help them to protect and care for each other's families. Jonathan was actually the legal heir to the throne, but because he recognized God's anointing on David, how did he prefer and honor David?

NUGGET: If we are not on guard, sometimes jealousy, ego and competition or possessiveness can sneak in on our friendships. Jonathan was the legal heir to the throne, but because he recognized God's hand and anointing on David and because he loved David, he was willing to humble himself and prefer David over himself. That takes maturity and God's love. Jonathan didn't want his own will for his life nor for David's; he wanted what God wanted.

Have you recognized God's hand, grace and anointing on your friends? If you find that they are called to something other than you, or more influential or more honored than you (as was the case with Jonathan and David), are you willing to put your own ego and desires aside and encourage your friend in God's will?

3. 2 Samuel 1:11-12, 25-27

Underline the phrase "Your love for me was wonderful, more wonderful than that of women."

> *Then David and all the men with him took hold of their clothes and tore them. They mourned and wept and fasted till evening for Saul and his son Jonathan, and for the army of the LORD and for the nation of Israel, because they had fallen by the sword.*
>
> *"How the mighty have fallen in battle! Jonathan lies slain on your heights. I grieve for you, Jonathan my brother; you were very dear to me. Your love for me was wonderful, more wonderful than that of women. How the mighty have fallen! The weapons of war have perished" (NIV).*

After Jonathan's death, David mourned deeply. What did David say about his friendship with Jonathan?

God wants to knit friendships together in Him. He wants us to enjoy the blessings that come from transparent and committed friendships, within healthy boundaries. I encourage you to pray and believe God for divine Jonathan-David friendships in your life. I have found that these types of friendships are rare. I thank God for blessing me with my own Jonathan-David type of friendships, as well as dozens of very rich and meaningful friendships on a variety of other levels.

NUGGET: Let's take a moment to talk about unhealthy relationships. Sometimes, people try to make the relationship that Jonathan and David had into something that it wasn't. They did not have a sexual, unhealthy or ungodly relationship. They were unashamed of their deep love for one another, the covenant they had made between them and their families, and the affection they shared.

How do you know when a relationship is unhealthy? The Bible tells us that when people begin to worship "created things" (each other) more than the Creator, they enter a danger zone. If you find that your thoughts are consumed with thinking about the other person in an obsessive, unnatural and unhealthy way, pay attention to this warning sign. The enemy would love for you to worship the people you love, and twist the love you feel for someone into idolatry and the worship of "created things."

Romans 1 describes what happens when people choose to invent their own ideas about God and live in a way that is contrary to His Word: "Because of this, God gave them over to shameful lusts. Even their women exchanged natural sexual relations for unnatural ones. In the same way the men also abandoned natural relations with women and were inflamed with lust for one another. Men committed shameful acts with other men, and received in themselves the due penalty for their error" (Romans 1:26-27, NIV)

Scriptures to Meditate On

*"For we have sworn friendship with each other in the name of the LORD,
saying, 'The LORD is witness between you and me"*

1 Samuel 20:42, NIV

*"I have called you friends,
for everything that I learned from my Father I have made known to you."*

John 15:15, NIV

Group Discussion

1. Describe any Jonathan-David type friendships the Lord has given you and the divine clickage that started your friendship.

2. Describe the level of commitment and communication in your Jonathan-David friendships. In what ways is it different than other friendships?

3. In addition to the joy and delight of a God-breathed friendship, have you recognized God's divine purpose in your friendship?

CHAPTER 4
Who's On Your Boat?

God-knit, God-connected friends are truly one of God's best gifts while we live on Planet Earth. Unfortunately, on the other side of the coin there are also dysfunctional and detrimental friendships. Are you troubled by unhealthy relationships? What toxic friendships are you enduring? What manipulative or co-dependant relationships are you trapped in? While God wants us to enjoy rich friendships, there are times when a relationship has run its course or taken an unhealthy turn, and we need to set boundaries or perhaps walk away.

Because believers feel obligated to turn the other cheek, walk in love, tolerate, go the extra mile, and love their enemies, they often put up with manipulative, toxic, unhealthy, abusive, co-dependent, draining, destructive, controlling and unhealthy relationships in the name of God's love. They put demands on themselves in relationships that even God himself does not expect. Certainly, there are times when we do need to walk in love, forgive, turn the other cheek, bless our enemies and be all things to all men in order to win them to Christ, but there are also times when we need to recognize the nature of a relationship and operate in truth and tough love. In their excellent book, *Boundaries*, Drs. Henry Cloud and John Townsend teach us how to set healthy boundaries with our parents, spouse, friends, co-workers and even ourselves.

What does the Bible say about the type of friends you need to steer clear of? The book of Jonah sheds an interesting light on taking inventory of those traveling on your boat.

Pastor Michael Pitts of Cornerstone Church in Toledo, Ohio, preaches one of the most enlightening sermons I've ever heard on dysfunctional relationships titled, "Get Off My Boat," from the book of Jonah. Let's look at this passage of

Scripture and see if we can glean some helpful insights regarding being set free from ungodly and unhealthy friendships.

Identify Friends Who Are Running from God

Jonah 1:1-3

Underline the phrase "Jonah ran away from the Lord."

> *The word of the LORD came to Jonah son of Amittai: "Go to the great city of Nineveh and preach against it, because its wickedness has come up before me." But Jonah ran away from the LORD and headed for Tarshish. He went down to Joppa, where he found a ship bound for that port. After paying the fare, he went aboard and sailed for Tarshish to flee from the LORD (NIV).*

What did God ask Jonah to do?

What was Jonah's response?

Describe the condition of a person who is disobeying and running away from God.

In your own life, do you have any friends who influence, control or manipulate your life in any way, who are also rebelling against God and His Word or are backslidden or prodigal in their faith?

NUGGET: People who are running from God are going in the wrong direction. Perhaps they are a non-believer who is running from Jesus and salvation, or maybe they are a believer who is choosing to disobey God and His Word and going their own way. Jonah was called by God to do something great but instead of running to God in obedience, he ran away from God and ended up being detrimental to those he came in contact with.

Identify People Who Cause Storms In Your Life

1. Jonah 1:3-4

Underline the phrases "a great wind" and "a violent storm."

> *But Jonah ran away from the LORD and headed for Tarshish. He went down to Joppa, where he found a ship bound for that port. After paying the fare, he went aboard and sailed for Tarshish to flee from the LORD. Then the LORD sent a great wind on the sea, and such a violent storm arose that the ship threatened to break up (NIV).*

When Jonah ran from the Lord, where did he end up?

What type of storm threatened the boat and passengers?

Think about your life; are you facing a storm? If so, reflect for a moment and identify when this storm began. Is there any connection to your storm and the relationships you have with people who are disobeying or running from or God's presence? In other words, have you become the friendship headquarters for backsliders, sinners and rebels? Perhaps the storm that has entered your life emotionally, mentally, spiritually and even physically has a direct connection to an unhealthy, ungodly relationship in your life. Perhaps it's time to do a boat inventory.

Who's on your boat relationally?

Are there any people in your life who consistently create a storm for you or your family—emotionally, mentally, financially, spiritually or physically?

2. Jonah 1:5-10

Underline the phrase "Jonah had gone below deck."

> *All the sailors were afraid and each cried out to his own god. And they threw the cargo into the sea to lighten the ship. But Jonah had gone below deck, where he lay down and fell into a deep sleep. The captain went to him and said, "How can you sleep? Get up and call on your god! Maybe he will take notice of us so that we will not perish." Then the sailors said to each other, "Come, let us cast lots to find out who is responsible for this calamity." They cast lots and the lot fell on Jonah. So they asked him, "Tell us, who is responsible for making all this trouble for us? What kind of work do you do? Where do you come from? What is your country? From what people are you?" He answered, "I am a Hebrew and I worship the LORD, the God of heaven, who made the sea and the dry land." This terrified them and they asked, "What have you done?" (They knew he was running away from the LORD, because he had already told them so.) (NIV).*

Who was responsible for the storm?

What was Jonah doing during the storm?

What were the sailors doing during the storm?

NUGGET: Have you ever noticed that Jonahs—people on the run from God—are often in a disobedient, co-dependent, dysfunctional, apathetic or lethargic state of being? They can be identified by their unwillingness to help others in the midst of the storm. Many times, other people try to bail Jonah out of his storms by rowing harder, spending their money and paying the price that Jonah is not willing to pay. In the story of Jonah, the boat owners were the ones using their energy and throwing their luggage and their wealth overboard, while disobedient Jonah was asleep in the bottom of the boat!

Notice that Jonah described himself as a Hebrew who worshipped the Lord of heaven. Often, Jonah is a backslidden and guilt-ridden Christian, running from obedience to God.

Identify the Solution for Calming the Storm

Jonah 1:11-15

Underline the phrases "What should we do to you to make the sea calm down for us?" and "Then they took Jonah and threw him overboard, and the raging sea grew calm."

The sea was getting rougher and rougher. So they asked him, "What should we do to you to make the sea calm down for us?" "Pick me up and throw me into the sea," he replied, "and it will become calm. I know that it is my fault that this great storm has come upon you." Instead, the men did their best to row back to land. But they could not, for the sea grew even wilder than before. Then they cried to the LORD, "Please LORD, please do not let us die for taking this man's life. Do not hold us accountable for killing an innocent man, for you, LORD, have done as you pleased." Then they took Jonah and threw him overboard, and the raging sea grew calm" (NIV).

People usually reach a breaking point in relationships—whether in marriage, friendship, with children, co-workers or employers. At some point, they can't take the relational storm anymore and they must make tough decisions.

In verse 11, what did the sailors ask Jonah?

In verse 12, what did Jonah say?

NUGGET: In order for peace to return to our lives, it is often going to require getting certain people off our boat! Reread verse 11 and meditate on the question they asked. We may have to throw people off our physical, emotional, mental or spiritual boat in order to find peace in our lives. We can't always literally throw people off our boat and out of our lives completely, especially if they are family. However, we can deny them access to our emotions, our minds, our time, our finances and certain areas of our lives.

In verse 13, what did the sailors do?

Why do we think we can "fix it"? Listen, if people don't want to be fixed, you can't fix them. If they don't want to obey and follow God, you can't make them. Rowing harder, preaching at them longer, taking on more of their responsibilities, covering for them, and making excuses for them will not fix them or calm your storm.

Describe the conflicted feelings the sailors were having according to verse 14.

On one hand, they wanted some calm back in their lives but on the other hand, they were feeling guilty about making Jonah responsible for his decisions and his life. How do you see this played out in modern society among friends and relatives?

In verse 15, when they finally threw Jonah off their boat and ended their relationship with him, what happened for them?

Are you feeding unhealthy relationships by staying in dysfunctional and co-dependant friendships? Is guilt or your desire to enable others causing you to be unwilling to throw Jonah off your boat? As a result, are you living a stormy life?

For your own peace of mind and heart, perhaps you need to prayerfully consider if there are any Jonahs on your boat, and then seek the Lord on how to throw them overboard!

Identify Healthy Relational Boundaries

You are not responsible for Jonah's life, success or future. In the end, Jonah repented, got right with God, and obeyed the Lord's will. Remember, God has a plan for the Jonahs in your life and at times, it may require you to set some healthy boundaries in order for them to come to their senses and follow God's will.

Jonah 1:16-17

Underline the phrase "the Lord provided a great fish."

> *"At this the men greatly feared the LORD, and they offered a sacrifice to the LORD and made vows to him. Now the LORD provided a great fish to swallow Jonah, and Jonah was in the belly of the fish three days and three nights" (NIV).*

What happened to the sailors' relationships with God when they threw Jonah overboard?

How did God take care of and provide for Jonah?

In the end, Jonah finally repented and obeyed God's will for his life. This never would have happened if the sailors had kept Jonah on the boat. In the same way, it's our job to throw all of our Jonah friends off our boat—our mental boat, our emotional boat, our spiritual boat and our physical boat. God is prepared to take care of Jonah, so let God do His work in the Jonahs in your life!

Seven Friends to Avoid Like the Plague

Now, let's get a closer look at some of the personality types we need to avoid like the plague.

#1. Tilly the Troublemaker

Proverbs 16:28

Underline the word "troublemaker." Circle the word "gossips."

Troublemakers start fights; gossips break up friendships (The Message).

What does this verse call those who like to start fights?

What type of person breaks up friendships?

Based on this verse, what type of people should you disassociate with?

The troublemaker is perverse and false. A troublemaker likes to stir up trouble, plant deception, tell falsehoods and pervert truth. Avoid this type of person, whether at the office, in the neighborhood, at school or in church. Troublemakers make trouble for you and everyone around them. Don't give troublemakers access to your boat.

#2. Penelope the Pretend Friend

Proverbs 18:24

Underline the phrase "pretend to be friends."

> *There are "friends" who pretend to be friends, but there is a friend who sticks closer than a brother (TLB).*

Pretend friends are also known as "convenient friends" and "fair-weather friends." They are there when friendship is convenient or in their best interest, but when the chips are down, they aren't around.

Describe a "pretend" friend.

Describe a "real" friend.

#3. Hilda the Hot Head

Proverbs 22:24-25

Underline the phrase "friends with a hot-tempered person."

> *Do not make friends with a hot-tempered person, do not associate with one easily angered, or you may learn their ways and get yourself ensnared (NIV).*

What kind of friendship are we to have with hot-tempered or angry people? Why?

Hot heads are everywhere—at the grocery store, your child's basketball or hockey game, driving cars, in line, at work and any place that a little patience is required. It's true, you become like those you hang around. Friends with a short fuse will eventually burn you. Hot heads and their tempers are contentious, contagious and infectious. Steer clear. Give them a big "Heave, ho, off my boat you go!"

#4. Gertrude the Gossip

Psalm 101:4-6

Underline the phrase "put a gag on the gossip."

> *The crooked in heart keep their distance; I refuse to shake hands with those who plan evil. I put a gag on the gossip who bad-mouths his neighbor; I can't stand arrogance. But I have my eye on salt-of-the-earth people—they're the ones I want working with me; Men and women on the straight and narrow—these are the ones I want at my side (The Message).*

According to verse 4, who do we refuse to be friends with?

According to verse 5, what do we gag and not tolerate?

What is gossip? Gossip is also translated as "talebearer" and comes from the Hebrew word nirgan. Its meaning includes: to murmur, to complain, to whisper, being a backbiter, a talebearer, to slander.[6]

---

6 *The Online Bible Thayer's Greek Lexicon* and *Brown Driver & Briggs Hebrew Lexicon*. Copyright ©1993 by Woodside Bible Fellowship, Ontario, Canada. Licensed from the Institute for Creation Research.

According to verse 6, what type of friends do we want?

Gossips create fires. Their murmuring, complaining, backbiting, slandering, whispers, embellishments, untruths and half-the-story lies break up friendships, hurt reputations and destroy people's lives. Proverbs 26:20 tells us, *"When you run out of wood, the fire goes out; when the gossip ends, the quarrel dies down" (The Message).* Don't add wood to the gossip's bonfire and the fire will go out.

If you've gotten in the bad habit of being "gossipy," just remember that gossips are not your friends because what they gossip about regarding other people in your presence, they will gossip about regarding you to others when you are not present. Don't be a gossip. Throw gossips off the boat of your life.

#5. Helga the Hell Raiser

Proverbs 1:10-15

Underline the phrase "raise some hell."

> *Dear friend, if bad companions tempt you, don't go along with them. If they say—"Let's go out and raise some hell. Let's beat up some old man, mug some old woman. Let's pick them clean and get them ready for their funerals. We'll load up on top-quality loot. We'll haul it home by the truck-load. Join us for the time of your life! With us, it's share and share alike!"—Oh, friend, don't give them a second look; don't listen to them for a minute (The Message).*

Our choice of friends begins at an early age, and is important at every season of life. Those we associate with have the potential to enrich or destroy our lives.

This passage describes the ungodly partiers, the mischievous, the rowdies, the vandals and the criminal. Don't be too quick to stereotype these types of people. It's not just the "classic trailer-trash, wife-beater, gang-bang, prison-types" that make up this group. You can find them in the popular "country-clubbing, martini-sipping, cigar-bar adultery crowd" just as often. The issue isn't your economic status, but the status of your heart's desire to live over the edge.

Have you had opportunities to hang with the wrong crowd?

What key decisions did you make to avoid going in the wrong direction?

In verse 15, what type of relationship does God want us to have with these types of people?

#6. Gretta the God-Rejecter

2 Corinthians 6:14-15

Underline the phrase "those who reject God."

> *Don't become partners with those who reject God. How can you make a partnership out of right and wrong? That's not partnership; that's war. Is light best friends with dark? Does Christ go strolling with the Devil? Do trust and mistrust hold hands? (The Message).*

We should not become friends with whom?

How can you be in the world and not of the world; befriending sinners like Jesus did, without becoming like those who reject God?

We are to let our lights shine before men, and we are to become all things to all men so that by all means we may lead them to Christ. We are to be a witness to those in darkness, but we are not to become best friends, partners or yoked together with unbelievers and those who reject God. A great passage on this balance is found in 1 Corinthians 9:19-22. There's a very good reason for living this way, which we will look at in the next verse of Scripture.

#7. Bertha and Her Bad Company

1 Corinthians 15:33

Underline the phrase "bad company."

> *Do not be misled: "Bad company corrupts good character" (NIV).*

This is the bottom line. What do bad friends do to you?

Bad company is bad news. The friends we associate with are a huge, huge, huge issue in terms of our own Christian life. We are either being influenced or we are being influencers, and when our primary friends do not share our faith in Jesus and our love for God and His Word, there is a good chance that their influence will have a negative effect on our own character. Think about other 'bad company"—people who whine, complain, are moody, negative and downers. Be careful that their company doesn't corrupt your good character!

NUGGET: One final thought: as parents, we spend years training, nurturing and protecting our children. We do our best to instill godly values and good character in our children, and yet one wrong friend can corrupt our children. How important is it that we pay attention to the friends our kids hang out with?

I hope you've been challenged and stirred up to review some of the friendships in your life. I pray that you will prayerfully consider the boundaries you need to set, and when necessary, throw some people off your boat!

Scriptures to Meditate On

Do not be misled:
"Bad company corrupts good character."

1 Corinthians 15:33, NIV

Do not make friends with a hot-tempered person,
do not associate with one easily angered,
or you may learn their ways and get yourself ensnared.

Proverbs 22:24-25, NIV

Group Discussion

1. Describe your experience with a Jonah and the storm you faced.

2. Describe how you handled the internal conflict or guilt trip as you threw your Jonah off the boat.

3. Which one of the "Seven Friends to Avoid Like the Plague" do you find the most challenging in your own life?

CHAPTER 5
Anatomy of a Friendship Famine

God said it in the beginning: It's not good for man to be alone. "No man is an island," to quote the Renaissance era poet and clergyman, John Donne. We weren't created to be an island.

The writer of Ecclesiastes understood a relational truth. *"I turned my head and saw yet another wisp of smoke on its way to nothingness: a solitary person, completely alone—no children, no family, no friends—yet working obsessively late into the night, compulsively greedy for more and more, never bothering to ask, 'Why am I working like a dog, never having any fun? And who cares?' More smoke. A bad business. It's better to have a partner than go it alone. Share the work, share the wealth. And if one falls down, the other helps, but if there's no one to help, tough! Two in a bed warm each other. Alone, you shiver all night. By yourself you're unprotected. With a friend you can face the worst. Can you round up a third? A three-stranded rope isn't easily snapped"* (Ecclesiastes 4:7-12, The Message).

Life is meant to be shared. Being a workaholic, hermit or loner is not God's best. He wants your life relationally rich! He'll knit you together with others and most importantly, with Him. God promises to set the solitary in families. If you are single, alone or lonely, God wants you to be relationally rich and He has a plan for helping you reap the blessing of rich friendships.

If you are feeling relationally challenged, alone or discouraged, don't despair. None of us have perfected the friendships in our lives. As I've already shared, I sowed a thirteen year "friendship famine" in my own life. I know what it's like to look around and say, "Hey, what happened to all my friends? All I see are my four toddlers, diapers, bottles, strollers and Legos!" I was in that busy season of mom-hood with preschoolers and didn't think I had time for meaningful friendships. I didn't sow friendship seeds and I didn't reap friends. Pretty plain, isn't it?

If you're experiencing a friendship famine, the good news is that your barren friendship field can grow. But first, let's look at the "bad news."

NUGGET: If we don't have a plethora of friends, is there a reason? We need to be honest with ourselves and with God. Is our friendship famine simply the result of our not sowing any friendship seeds or are we doing something to undermine potential friendships? Are we doing anything that would cause friends to avoid or run from us? Are we hard to be around? Self-absorbed? Critical? A stick in the mud? Boring? A whiner? Face it, no one wants to be around a downer or those who are having constant pity parties. Are we making ourselves enjoyable to be around? A pleasure to work with? Easy to talk to? We have a responsibility to exhibit godly qualities that people enjoy being around. If you identify areas of weakness in your own friendship quotient, seek the Lord and adjust. Now, let's take a look at the good news!

If You Want to Have Friends, Sow Friendliness

Are you looking for a big harvest of friendship? Ready to plant a bag of "friendship seeds?" If you've experienced famine in your relationships, it's time to sow and reap. It's easier than you think.

Let's look at the law of seedtime and harvest that God has established.

1. Genesis 8:22

   Underline the phrase "seedtime and harvest."

   While the earth remains, seedtime and harvest, cold and heat, winter and summer, and day and night shall not cease (NKJV).

What four things did God say would not cease?

2. Genesis 26:1, 12-14

   Underline the words "famine," "Isaac planted" and "the same year reaped."

   Now there was a famine in the land . . .

   Isaac planted crops in that land and the same year reaped a hundredfold, because the LORD blessed him. The man became rich, and his wealth continued to grow until he became very wealthy. He had so many flocks and herds and servants that the Philistines envied him (NIV).

   In verse 1, what was Isaac experiencing?

   In verse 12, what did Isaac do in the midst of a famine?

   In verses 12-14, what happened to Isaac?

   Do you believe that if you sow "friendship crops" in the midst of a friendship famine, God will cause you to reap and become very rich and wealthy in relationships?

3. Galatians 6:7-10

Underline the sentence "What a person plants, he will harvest."

> *Don't be misled: No one makes a fool of God. What a person plants, he will harvest. The person who plants selfishness, ignoring the needs of others—ignoring God—harvests a crop of weeds. All he'll have to show for his life is weeds! But the one who plants in response to God, letting God's Spirit do the growth work in him, harvests a crop of real life, eternal life. So let's not allow ourselves to get fatigued doing good. At the right time we will harvest a good crop if we don't give up, or quit (The Message).*

If we plant selfishness, what will we reap?

If we plant godly seeds, what will we reap?

What does verse 9 tell us about patience?

4. Proverbs 18:24

Underline the phrase "be friendly."

> *A man who has friends must himself be friendly, but there is a friend who sticks closer than a brother (NKJV).*

If you want to have friends, what must you be?

How can you sow "friendliness" into the people in your life?

Sometimes, all it takes is little things like smiling, saying hello, asking questions and taking the initiative to show you are genuinely interested in others.

* **NUGGET: If you want a friendship harvest, you will have to take the initiative. If you've ever attended church, gone to the neighborhood cookout or the office party and left feeling like "no one was friendly" at the event, it's time to take a look in the mirror! Don't put the responsibility for your friendship harvest on the shoulders of others; don't expect them to reach out and include you unless you are willing to reach out first and take the initiative in being friendly. If you sit back and wait for others to come up to you, to include you, to get to know you, or become your best friend, you may wait a long time.**

Perhaps you feel insecure in reaching out to or in planting friendship seeds. How do you break the friendship famine cycle? Here are some seeds you can begin to plant into the lives of those around you.

Plant Seeds of Genuine Interest in Others

Sow interest! Be interested.

As Dale Carnegie once said, "You can make more friends in two months by becoming interested in other people than you can in two years of trying to get other people interested in you." I believe this is the most misunderstood secret to mutually enjoyable personal relationships. Think about it. When was the last time you took note of the affairs, challenges, projects, dreams, events and dynamics of the people in your world and asked them a meaningful question about their life? And then continued to show interest in their lives by asking several good follow-up questions?

If this type of conversation has not taken place in a long time, you are sowing a friendship famine. If your most recent conversations with family, friends or co-workers have revolved around you telling them stories about you, you might want to do a 180 and start asking questions that show you're interested in them. Being interested in others goes against our selfish nature, so remember; the key to being interesting is to be interested!

Showing disinterest in someone is worse than showing dislike. Dislike says, "I just don't like you." Disinterest says, "I don't care about you." Being ignored is worse than being insulted. Ignoring someone says, "You don't exist." Insulting someone says, "You exist and here are your flaws." If you avoid others, you are telling them, "I notice you, and I don't want to be near you." If you are indifferent toward others, you are saying, "You don't impress me in any way. You are nothing to me." Which is worse? Both speak friendship famine.

If we sow interest in others in an atmosphere of love and acceptance, we'll find a whole new level of rich relationships open up to us. Let's see what God's Word has to say about this.

1. Philippians 2:19-22

    Underline the way Timothy sowed acceptance into the lives of the Philippians.

    > But I hope and trust in the Lord Jesus soon to send Timothy to you, so that I may also be encouraged and cheered by learning news of you. For I have no one like him [no one of so kindred a spirit] who will be so genuinely interested in your welfare and devoted to your interests. For the others all seek [to advance] their own interests, not those of Jesus Christ (the Messiah). But Timothy's tested worth you know, how as a son with his father he has toiled with me zealously in [serving and helping to advance] the good news (the Gospel) (AMP).

The Living Bible says it this way:

> *There is no one like Timothy for having a real interest in you; everyone else seems to be worrying about his own plans and not those of Jesus Christ.*

According to verse 20, what made Timothy stand out?

Are people like Timothy hard to find or commonplace?

What was Timothy truly interested in?

What were others interested in?

In what ways could you be more like Timothy to the people in your life?

2. Philippians 2:4

Underline the word that describes our approach with others.

> *Don't just think about your own affairs, but be interested in others, too, and in what they are doing (TLB).*

What does this tell us concerning our interest in our own lives?

What part of others' lives are we to be interested in?

The way to show interest is simply asking questions. When you ask others questions about themselves and the things they are doing—their hobbies, their dreams and goals—it demonstrates that you genuinely care.

3. John 16:5-6

    Underline the thing that Jesus rebuked.

    > *But now I am going away to the one who sent me; and none of you seems interested in the purpose of my going; none wonders why. Instead you are only filled with sorrow (TLB).*

    What were the disciples not interested in?

    What consumed their interest?

    In what ways are we often consumed with our own "pity parties" and not aware of the interests of those around us?

4. Zechariah 7:6

Underline the thing that God is interested in.

> *And when you held feasts, was that for me? Hardly. You're interested in religion, I'm interested in people (The Message).*

What's the bottom line on what God is interested in?

When you and I show an interest in others, we are acting like God. We stand out, because as the Apostle Paul said, there are not many people like Timothy who will naturally care for the interests of others. Let's be the kind of people who overcome our own needs by sowing into the lives of others. As a result, we will reap a harvest!

Plant Seeds of Transparency and Vulnerability

Most people want to feel noticed, liked, accepted, appreciated and approved of by the people important to them. We want people to want us. We have a need to know and be known. Secular behavior and motivation experts like Abraham Maslow teach us that self-disclosure is a basic need of human beings. Once certain basic needs are met in a person's life, they have a need to disclose personal information as this creates a feeling of closeness between people.

I like what Christian author and founder of the Family Dynamics Institute, Joe Beam, said in his article "Becoming Vulnerable" (http://www.familydynamics. net, used by permission of the author):

> *"Removing all masks to let another see who we really are ('warts and all') means risking everything in that relationship. If the other person doesn't accept us when they encounter our undisguised selves, we feel absolute rejection. We likely won't continue the relationship, even if the other person wants to, because we know that he or she has seen the true*

us and been repulsed by the discovery. So how do we grow past that fear and decide to reveal our true selves? We do it in stages. We start by sharing facts that are non-threatening; facts that we feel won't be reacted to negatively. As we share those innocuous facts of our lives (e.g. "I was born in the USA,") we register every reaction of the person to whom we share. Any lack of interest or hint of displeasure on their part causes us to stop the process. We're certainly not going to reveal potentially threatening facts (e.g. "When I was a kid I was arrested,") if we note any disinterest or rejection as we share innocuous facts. On the other hand, as we register interest and acceptance we tend to reveal more threatening facts. We can become so trusting of the seemingly uncondi-tional acceptance of the other person that we tell him or her things about ourselves we've never told anyone."

The Apostle Paul was good at sharing his heart, being vulnerable with others, and planting these types of seeds into the lives of others. Let's see what we can learn about sowing vulnerability and transparency seeds.

1.   2 Corinthians 6:11-13

Underline the way Paul was vulnerable.

> *We have spoken freely to you, Corinthians, and opened wide our hearts to you. We are not withholding our affection from you, but you are withholding yours from us. As a fair ex-change—I speak as to my children—open wide your hearts also (NIV).*

> *Oh, my dear Corinthian friends! I have told you all my feel-ings; I love you with all my heart. Any coldness still between us is not because of any lack of love on my part but because your love is too small and does not reach out to me and draw me in. I am talking to you now as if you truly were my very own children. Open your hearts to us! Return our love (TLB).*

How did Paul communicate?

How does this passage describe self-disclosure on Paul's part?

What does Paul encourage the believers to do?

2. 1 Thessalonians 2:8

    Underline the things that Paul shares with the believers.

    > *Because we loved you so much, we were delighted to share with you not only the gospel of God but our lives as well (NIV).*

    How did Paul describe his feelings for these believers?

    In your relationships, do you share both the gospel and your own life?

I hope this lesson has inspired and encouraged you to reach out to others. Get ready for a rich harvest of God-knit friendships as you sow friendship seeds!

Scriptures to Meditate On

So this is my prayer: that your love will flourish and that you will not only love much but well. Learn to love appropriately. You need to use your head and test your feelings so that your love is sincere and intelligent, not sentimental gush. Live a lover's life, circumspect and exemplary, a life Jesus will be proud of: bountiful in fruits from the soul, making Jesus Christ attractive to all, getting everyone involved in the glory and praise of God.

Philippians 1:9-11, The Message

Don't be misled: No one makes a fool of God. What a person plants, he will harvest. The person who plants selfishness, ignoring the needs of others—ignoring God!—harvests a crop of weeds. All he'll have to show for his life is weeds! But the one who plants in response to God, letting God's Spirit do the growth work in him, harvests a crop of real life, eternal life. So let's not allow ourselves to get fatigued doing good. At the right time we will harvest a good crop if we don't give up, or quit.

Galatians 6:7-9, The Message

Group Discussion

1. Describe the law of sowing and reaping in areas of your life. What role does the seed, soil, and patience play?

2. Describe the power of showing interest in others. Share a story of someone showing interest in your life.

3. Describe the challenge of being transparent or vulnerable and the risks involved. What things are appropriate to share and what things need to be avoided?

CHAPTER 6
A Friend of God

God is looking for friends! Did you know that? You may have a wonderful husband, children you love and cherish, the dearest girl friends in the world and a God-knit Jonathan-David friendship, but there is still likely going to be a place inside of you that longs for Someone to know and understand the deepest part of you. The Bible says, *"Deep calls to deep,"* which means the deepest part of us is calling out and only a deep friendship with God can answer back. All the human friendships God sends us are simply the "icing on the cake," but He's the cake! Yes, He's the cake! So, let's end this study on friendship by talking about the friendship that matters most: being a friend of God.

Blaise Pascal, the French mathematician and physicist said, *"There is a God-shaped vacuum in the heart of every person and it can never be filled by any created thing. It can only be filled by God, made known through Jesus Christ."* It's true. It's true!

It's something to ponder, isn't it? When we confess Him as Lord, Jesus calls us friends. Think about that. How well do we know Him as our Friend?

You Can Be God's Friend

Perhaps you're a believer and Jesus is your Lord and Savior, but do you also know Him as your Friend? You can.

Let's begin our study by looking at what the Bible says about being God's friend.

1. Psalm 25:14

Underline the phrase "friendship with God."

> *Friendship with God is reserved for those who reverence him. With them alone he shares the secrets of his promises (TLB).*

Who gets to be God's friend?

What does God share with His friends?

Listen to how the Message Bible relays this verse:

> *God-friendship is for God-worshipers; they are the ones he confides in.*

How would you describe the components of being God's friend?

2. Psalm 34:15

Underline the phrase "his friends."

> *God keeps an eye on his friends, his ears pick up every moan and groan (The Message).*

What does God do for His friends?

It's nice to know we have friends in high places! We're never alone.

3. Micah 7:5-7

Underline the friends you potentially cannot trust and the friend you can always count on.

> *Don't trust your neighbor, don't confide in your friend. Watch your words, even with your spouse. Neighborhoods and families are falling to pieces. The closer they are—sons, daughters, in-laws—the worse they can be. Your own family is the enemy. But me, I'm not giving up. I'm sticking around to see what GOD will do. I'm waiting for God to make things right. I'm counting on God to listen to me (The Message).*

Nugget: People are going to let you down; God has designed it that way. There are times when even our best friend, husband and family will disappoint us, intentionally or unintentionally. No human being is designed to be our "all in all."

When every human friend you have has let you down, what Friend can you count on and why?

4. Romans 5:9-11

Underline the phrase "this amazing friendship with God."

> *Now that we are set right with God by means of this sacrificial death, the consummate blood sacrifice, there is no longer a question of being at odds with God in any way. If, when we were at our worst, we were put on friendly terms with God by the sacrificial death of his Son, now that we're at our best, just think of how our lives will expand and deepen by means of his resurrection life! Now that we have actually received*

*this amazing friendship with God, we are no longer content to
simply say it in plodding prose. We sing and shout our praises
to God through Jesus, the Messiah (The Message).*

According to verses 9-10, what has happened to our friendship with God
as a result of Jesus' death on the cross?

According to verse 11, what does being a friend of God inspire our hearts
to do?

**NUGGET: When we have a personal relationship with God through
Jesus Christ, when His friendship is real to us and not just a religious duty, we can't help but talk about Him. Think about your love
life. If you're married, did you keep it a big secret when you fell in
love with your husband? No! You light up when you think about your
husband. You want to "show him off" to all your girlfriends, right?
You want to tell everyone about your husband —how good-look-
ing, caring, smart, athletic or funny he is, right? If that is the natural response in our most loving human relationships, shouldn't we
be even more enthusiastic to share our friendship with the Lord?**

4. 2 Corinthians 13:14

Underline the phrases "amazing grace," "extravagant love" and "intimate
friendship."

*The amazing grace of the Master, Jesus Christ, the extrava-
gant love of God, the intimate friendship of the Holy Spirit, be
with all of you (The Message).*

Isn't it wonderful to know that we can have a personal friendship with each person in the Godhead—God the Father, Jesus the Master, and the Holy Spirit?

What does our friendship with the Master, Jesus, bring to our lives?

What does our friendship with God the Father fill us with?

What does our friendship with the Holy Spirit look like?

Abraham Was God's Friend

1. James 2:23

    Underline the phrase "the friend of God."

    > *And so it happened just as the Scriptures say: "Abraham be-lieved God, and God counted him as righteous because of his faith." He was even called the friend of God (NLT).*

    According to this verse, what was Abraham called?

    What caused Abraham to be called "the friend of God"?

Simple, right? Faith pleases God. Though we haven't seen Him, we love Him and He calls us friend. Our friendship with God begins with belief.

Do you believe God?

Do you take Him at His Word?

Describe a time when you had to choose between believing God and His Word rather than your own thoughts, circumstances or the words of others.

2. Genesis 18:19

Underline the phrase "Yes, I've settled on him."

> *Yes, I've settled on him as the one to train his children and future family to observe GOD'S way of life, live kindly and generously and fairly, so that GOD can complete in Abraham what he promised him (The Message).*

Here, we get a little more insight into what God liked about Abraham. What qualities did God see in Abraham?

What role does trust play in a friendship?

Can God trust you to keep His Word?

Do you trust God to perform His Word?

3. Isaiah 41:8

Underline the phrase "he was my friend."

> *But as for you, O Israel, you are mine, my chosen ones; for*
> *you are Abraham's family, and he was my friend (TLB).*

It's nice being related to people who are friends with God! Through our faith
in Jesus Christ, the Bible says we've become part of Abraham's family and
heirs of all that God promised him. *"So those now who live by faith are bless-*
ed along with Abraham, who lived by faith—this is no new doctrine!" (Gala-
tians 3:9-10, The Message).

Since we are related to Abraham through Jesus Christ, what does God
call us?

If you study Abraham's life you will find that because of his friendship
with God, also known as a covenant, everything that belonged to Abraham was God's, and everything that belonged to God was Abraham's.
Who do you think got the better deal?

CLICK

Moses Was God's Friend

1. Exodus 33:11

   Underline the phrase "his friend."

   > *So the LORD spoke to Moses face to face, as a man speaks to his friend (NKJV).*

   How did God speak with Moses?

2. Exodus 33:14-19

   Underline the word "Presence" and the phrase "I am pleased with you and I know you by name."

   > *The LORD replied, "My Presence will go with you, and I will give you rest." Then Moses said to him, "If your Presence does not go with us, do not send us up from here. How will anyone know that you are pleased with me and with your people unless you go with us? What else will distinguish me and your people from all the other people on the face of the earth?" And the LORD said to Moses, "I will do the very thing you have asked, because I am pleased with you and I know you by name." Then Moses said, "Now show me your glory." And the LORD said, "I will cause all my goodness to pass in front of you, and I will proclaim my name, the LORD, in your presence. I will have mercy on whom I will have mercy, and I will have compassion on whom I will have compassion" (NIV).*

   The reality of God's Presence and friendship can and should be tangible in our lives.

In verses 15 and 18, what did Moses say he couldn't live without?

In verse 16, what did Moses say that God's Presence demonstrated?

In verses 14, 17 and 19, the Lord speaks very personally to Moses. What did He say?

How does the thought that God would know your name impact you?

How would you describe the idea of having God's Presence in your life?

3. Exodus 34:5-7

    Underline the phrase "the Lord came down."

    > Then the LORD came down in the cloud and stood there with
    > him and proclaimed his name, the LORD. And he passed in
    > front of Moses, proclaiming, "The LORD, the LORD, the com-
    > passionate and gracious God, slow to anger, abounding in
    > love and faithfulness, maintaining love to thousands, and for-
    > giving wickedness, rebellion and sin" (NIV).

When God's presence, goodness and friendship were tangibly manifested to Moses, what character traits did the Lord reveal about the type of God and friend He is?

Enoch Was God's Friend

1. Genesis 5:22-24

   Underline the phrase "Enoch walked faithfully with God."

   > *And after he became the father of Methuselah, Enoch walked faithfully with God 300 years and had other sons and daughters. Altogether, Enoch lived 365 years. Enoch walked faithfully with God; then he was no more, because God took him away (NIV).*

   It's hard to grasp the reality that people lived to be 365 years old! What did Enoch do during his 300+ years?

   In your own words, what does it mean to "walk with God"?

2. Hebrews 11:5

   Underline the phrase "he pleased God."

   > *By an act of faith, Enoch skipped death completely. "They looked all over and couldn't find him because God had taken him." We know on the basis of reliable testimony that before he was taken "he pleased God" (The Message).*

God was pleased with Enoch. They walked together for hundreds of years. They had a rich history of friendship during Enoch's life. Enoch and the Lord were so close that God didn't want to spend another day with Enoch living on earth and God living in heaven. So God sent "Two Angels and a Chariot" and transferred Enoch to heaven, without facing death!

What did God do to Enoch?

What event does that sound like?

Jesus Calls You His Friend

1. Proverbs 18:24

    Underline the words "friends" and "friendly."

    A man who has friends must himself be friendly, but there is a friend who sticks closer than a brother (NKJV).

    Who is the Friend who sticks closer than a brother?

    What does that mean to you?

2. Luke 12:31-32

    Underline the phrase "You're my dearest friends."

107

Steep yourself in God-reality, God-initiative, God-provisions. You'll find all your everyday human concerns will be met. Don't be afraid of missing out. You're my dearest friends! The Father wants to give you the very kingdom itself (The Message).

In verse 32, what does Jesus call those who believe and follow Him?

In your own words, what does a friendship with Jesus look like?

In verse 31, what does He tell His friends to do?

NUGGET: Can you see that Jesus isn't talking about a casual friendship? He's talking about "steeping" yourself—saturating and marinating your life with God realities! The Lord wants a close, intense and dynamic friendship with His people.

3. John 15:12-15

Underline the phrase "I have called you friends."

My command is this: Love each other as I have loved you. Greater love has no one than this: to lay down one's life for one's friends. You are my friends if you do what I command. I no longer call you servants, because a servant does not know his master's business. Instead, I have called you friends, for everything that I learned from my Father I have made known to you (NIV).

In verses 14 and 15, what does Jesus call His followers?

In verse 13, what did Jesus say was the greatest thing a person can do for a friend?

Jesus proved His love for us when He laid down His life on the cross. In verse 12, what does Jesus want us to do to others?

While we call Him Lord, Savior and Master, He calls us His friends.

Don't Fake It

Let's end this study with an encouragement to be genuine in your relationship with the Lord. God is looking for real friends—those who really want Him. Are you one of those people?

1. Psalm 50:16-23

    Underline the phrases "talking like we are good friends" and "it's the praising life that honors me."

    Next, God calls up the wicked: "What are you up to, quoting my laws, talking like we are good friends? You never answer the door when I call; you treat my words like garbage. If you find a thief, you make him your buddy; adulterers are your friends of choice. Your mouth drools filth; lying is a serious art form with you. You stab your own brother in the back, rip off your little sister. I kept a quiet patience while you did these things; you thought I went along with your game. I'm calling you on the carpet, now, laying your wickedness out in plain sight. Time's up for playing fast and loose with me. I'm ready to pass sentence, and there's no help in sight! It's the praising life that honors me. As soon as you set your foot on the Way, I'll show you my salvation" (The Message).

In verse 16, what did God say about these religious fakes?

In verse 17, how did God describe His relationship with these phonies; what did they do with Him and His Word?

In verses 18-20, what did God know about these people?

In verses 21-22, God's patience with these people was up. What did God say?

In verse 23, what type of friend is God looking for?

2. James 4:4

Underline the phrases "friendship with the world" and "friend of the world."

You adulterous people, don't you know that friendship with the world means enmity against God? Therefore, anyone who chooses to be a friend of the world becomes an enemy of God (NIV).

We get to choose: friendship with the world or friendship with God. How would you describe friendship with the world?

If we choose friendship with the world rather than friendship with God, what do we become?

How would you describe friendship with God?

If we choose friendship with the world (the rule of lust and pride, according to 1 John 2:15-17), what does that say about our relationship with God?

NUGGET: God loves the world so much He sent His Son to die on the cross. At the same time, friendship with the world is rebuked because it takes the place reserved for the Lord alone. Friendship with the world is described in 1 John 2:15-17, "*Do not love this world nor the things it offers you, for when you love the world, you do not have the love of the Father in you. For the world offers only a craving for physical pleasure, a craving for everything we see, and pride in our achievements and possessions. These are not from the Father, but are from this evil world. And this world is fading away, along with everything that people crave. But anyone who does what pleases God will live forever"* (NLT). Notice, friendship with the world or friendship with God is something that we get to choose. God will not force Himself on us; He gives us a free will to choose.

Are you a friend of God? I hope so. Perhaps as you've looked at this lesson, you realize that although you know some things about God, you do not know Him personally. If that's you, today is the day that can change! You can begin a vital, dynamic relationship with God through Jesus Christ by simply turning from your sins and inviting Jesus into your life. Pray this prayer to begin your friendship with God:

"Dear God, I humble my heart before You. I want to turn from a sinful life and turn to You. Jesus, I invite You to be the Lord of my life, to forgive and cleanse me from every sin I've committed. I want to know You. I want a real, genuine friendship with You. Help me to walk with You every day. In Jesus' Name. Amen."

Scriptures to Meditate On

A man who has friends must himself be friendly,
But there is a friend who sticks closer than a brother.

Proverbs 18:24, NKJV

The LORD is a friend to those who fear him.
He teaches them his covenant.

Psalm 25:14, NLT

Group Discussion

1. Which of these words describes the way you have viewed God?

   • Angry Distant God

   • Spiritual "Santa Claus"

   • Mean Judge

   • Grandfather Figure

   • Impersonal Force

   • Genuine Friend

   • God Who Winks at Sin

   • Loving Father

   • Merciful Forgiver

2. Describe the difference between knowing "about" someone and knowing someone personally.

3. Describe any changes you intend to make in your life to cultivate your friendship with God.

ABOUT THE AUTHOR
Beth Jones

Beth Jones and her husband Jeff are the founders and senior pastors of Valley Family Church in Kalamazoo, Michigan, planted in 1991 and named by Outreach magazine as one of the fastest growing churches in America in 2009 and 2010. They also lead Jeff and Beth Jones Ministries, an organization dedicated to helping people *get the basics*. Beth and Jeff have four children who are all involved in leadership and ministry.

Beth grew up in Lansing, Michigan, and was raised as a Catholic. At the end of her freshman year in college, she came into a personal relationship with Christ through the testimony of her roommate. It was there, at age 19, that she realized God's plan for her to preach and teach the gospel through writing and speaking. She has been following that call ever since.

Beth is the author of 20 books, including the popular *Getting a Grip on the Basics* series, which is being used by thousands of churches in America and has been translated into over a dozen foreign languages and used around the world. She also writes *The Basics Daily Devo*, a free daily edevotional for thousands of subscribers.

The heart of Beth's message is simple: *"I exist to help people get the basics!"* Through her practical, down-to-earth teaching, she inspires people to enjoy an authentic relationship with Jesus, to take Him at His Word, and to reach their greatest God-given potential!

Beth attended Boston University in Boston, Massachusetts and received her ministry training at Rhema Bible Training Center in Tulsa, Oklahoma.

For more spiritual growth resources or to connect with Beth, please visit:

www.valleyfamilychurch.org

www.jeffandbethjones.com

www.facebook.com/jeffandbethjones

www.twitter.com/bethjones

www.instagram.com/bethjones

PRAYER OF SALVATION

God loves you—no matter who you are, no matter what your past. God loves you so much that He gave His one and only begotten Son for you. The Bible tells us that "...whoever believes in Him shall not perish but have eternal life" (John 3:16 NIV). Jesus laid down His life and rose again so that we could spend eternity with Him in heaven and experience His absolute best on earth. If you would like to receive Jesus into your life, say the following prayer out loud and mean it from your heart.

Heavenly Father, I come to You admitting that I am a sinner. Right now, I choose to turn away from sin, and I ask You to cleanse me of all unrighteousness. I believe that Your Son, Jesus, died on the cross to take away my sins. I also believe that He rose again from the dead so that I might be forgiven of my sins and made righteous through faith in Him. I call upon the name of Jesus Christ to be the Savior and Lord of my life. Jesus, I choose to follow You and ask that You fill me with the power of the Holy Spirit. I declare that right now I am a child of God. I am free from sin and full of the righteousness of God. I am saved in Jesus' name. Amen.

If you prayed this prayer to receive Jesus Christ as your Savior for the first time, please contact us on the Web at **www.harrisonhouse.com** to receive a free book.

Or you may write to us at

Harrison House • P.O. Box 35035 • Tulsa, Oklahoma 74153

The Harrison House Vision

Proclaiming the truth and the power

Of the Gospel of Jesus Christ

With excellence;

Challenging Christians to

Live victoriously,

Grow spiritually,

Know God intimately.